WHO GOES THERE?

THE AUTHOR

WHO GOES THERE?

BY

SIR ARCHIBALD HURD

With 16 Illustrations

HUTCHINSON & CO. (Publishers), LTD.
LONDON :: AND :: MELBOURNE

MADE AND PRINTED IN GREAT BRITAIN
AT GAINSBOROUGH PRESS, ST. ALBANS,
BY FISHER, KNIGHT AND CO., LTD.

On Saturday night when any of His Majesty's ships is at sea, the toast of "The King" is honoured in every wardroom —the officers remaining seated in accordance with a custom dating back to the time when there was insufficient headroom for standing in the ships of wood. And then comes the toast "Sweethearts and Wives," a voice at the end of the table usually expressing the hope—"And may they never meet."

It is fifty years since I first met my wife and she is still my sweetheart, to whom this collection of memories is gratefully dedicated.

In times of peace and war, the three toasts in every home might well be "The King: God bless him," "Sweethearts and Wives" and "The Seamen of our Race who stand always between us and starvation."

September 19*th*, 1941.

FOREWORD

THESE pages deal mainly with people who, at one time or another, were unpopular because they would not, or could not, reply to the challenge "Who Goes There?" with the password of the hour which the majority of their fellow-countrymen, represented in the newspapers, demanded of them.

Statesmen like Mr. H. H. Asquith, Lord Haldane and Mr. Reginald McKenna, sailors such as Lord Fisher and Lord Jellicoe, and some others who forfeited, for a time at least, the sympathy of those whom they sought to serve, reappear in this volume. Shipowners also move across the stage. Who so unpopular as they?—until it was discovered in the autumn of 1939 that the nation needed merchant ships in order that it might fight in the war against evil which has mobilised the strength of the English-speaking world, divorced otherwise by the sea. Finally, there are journalists, some of them famous and some of them little known, with whom I have associated.

As Prime Minister, Mr. Asquith was condemned because he often told impatient questioners to "Wait and see"; Lord Haldane was never forgiven his confession, "My spiritual home is in Germany"; Mr. McKenna refused to respond, at the time of the "Dreadnought" controversy in 1909, to the cry "We want eight and we won't wait"; Lord Fisher was criticised because he had said that "Favouritism is the secret of efficiency" and had told the people of this country to "Sleep quietly in your beds," while Lord Jellicoe, who was known as "Hellfire Jack" in his young days, was believed to have been too cautious when, as Commander-in-Chief of the Grand Fleet, he met the German High Seas Fleet off Jutland.

And so it was with others who figure in this volume. They got out of touch with public opinion and for the time, at least, lost the confidence of those whom they were serving in their respective spheres with singleness of purpose and devotion, and, as the nation must now realise, to its salvation from the tyranny of the enemy.

CONTENTS

DEDICATION

FOREWORD

LIST OF ILLUSTRATIONS

CHAPTER I

THE BEGINNING OF THINGS

I DO not flatter myself that anyone is interested in my birth or teething troubles. When I reread "David Copperfield," as I do each year, I regret that so many pages are devoted to the hero's birth and the doings of his very foolish mother, which might have been given up to that delightful couple Betsy Trotwood and Mr. Dick. As I close the volume, I have some curiosity to know how David and Agnes got on in their married life. Was his spirit tamed without being broken, and did she always preserve that imperturbability of temper which made her more than angelic? Angels sometimes rebel and fall out of Heaven, if reliance can be placed on the meagre biographical details of Lucifer which have come to us down the ages.

But the memories of my life, which are mainly concerned with people of various degrees of eminence, should, I suppose, have some sort of background.

The name of Hurd is common in the United States and in Canada. On first entering Boston, I noticed it in very big letters over a pawnbroker's shop. But one seldom comes across it in this country. The family has, however, made contributions to theology and hydrography; for the former, Richard Hurd (1720–1808), successively Bishop of Lichfield, Coventry and Worcester, who declined the preferment to Canterbury because he considered himself unequal to the position, was responsible; for the latter Captain Thomas Hurd (1757–1823). This officer, after serving at sea and gaining a reputation for his ocean surveys, became Hydrographer of the Royal Navy, serving at the Admiralty from 1808 until his death. Of the two men, I think the naval captain has the better claim to fame. Dr. Hurd left behind him volumes of sermons, which were well thought of at the time, but now are read by nobody, and he added a beautiful library to Hartlebury Castle for the housing of the books which had been collected by Pope and Warburton, which no one uses. Dr. Johnson declared that "Hurd, sir, is a man whose acquaintance is a valuable acquisition"—a generous tribute, for the Bishop was a Whig and Johnson hated Whigs. The bishop is almost forgotten. He was known, according to Madame D'Arbley, as "The Beauty of Holiness." The naval captain's fame, on the other hand, is perpetuated by Cape Hurd on the Canadian Coast and by Hurd Deep in the English Channel —enduring reminders of his pioneer work when the importance of surveying the seas and oceans of the world and making them safer for navigation was only just beginning to be appreciated.

My father practised as a solicitor when I became conscious of his existence. He was a Victorian of great dignity and fine presence. He was always dressed in black West of England broadcloth, and usually wore a silk hat, somewhat resembling that of a bishop. In later life, he had beautiful white hair and a noble beard, which was also white. His only rival when he lived at Highgate in the 'nineties was Sir John Glover, the outstanding tramp shipowner of his day. They had the same barber.

My mother led a life comparable with that of Anthony Trollope's mother, whose experiences he has described in "An Autobiography," a volume which admirably reflects some of the sidelights of life in the early years of last century. It is a book which every young woman of this more leisurely age should read. My own mother, with six sons and no daughter to help her, was one of the most capable of women. Blessed is the man whose mother is his first heroine!

I recall our first home—it seemed a mansion in my childish eyes—with its hall laid in alternate squares of black and white marble, from which a wide, curving stair-case ascended to the bedrooms, its stables and its large garden. It was flush with the street in the village of Berkeley, made famous by the murder of King Edward II in its castle. The village lies in the Vale of Berkeley, "which consists," as I have since learned, "of rich meadow pasture land on a deep, flat loam," and was, and may still be, "celebrated for its dairies and Double Gloucester cheese." Berkeley has given to the world one benefactor in Dr. Edward Jenner, who conquered smallpox, once the scourge of the country. The son of the vicar of the village, he was the favourite pupil of John Hunter and was later employed by Sir Joseph Banks to arrange the zoological specimens which that scientist had brought back from Captain Cook's first voyage of discovery. Edward Jenner, though he was only the village doctor, was a remarkable man—a student, especially of the habits of birds, a musician who could play both the flute and the violin, a writer of prose and something of a poet. But this is all forgotten. He is remembered only as the doctor who studied cow-pox among the herds in the countryside and at last startled the medical world with his pamphlets, which worked a revolution in medical practice. This was the man who made his living as a "G.P." under the shadow of Berkeley Castle, the seat since the thirteenth century of the richest and most powerful family in Gloucestershire. As a child I had a dread of the castle, as the place where in a dark dungeon Edward II had been murdered after every effort had been made, in vain, to infect him with a deadly disease.

I have since visited this first home of my family, and discovered that it was, in fact, quite a modest house. I wished to walk again in Berkeley Park, where I played as a little boy and of which I have a painful memory. A squirrel inconsiderately bit my finger because I tried to catch it by the tail. This beautifully wooded pleasure ground, I was told, was closed to the public. I left Berkeley a convinced Communist—for that day at least.

We were miles removed from a railway. No madman had thought of the internal combustion engine, bringing in its train the motor-car to ruin our country solitudes, and the cursed aeroplane, with its bombs. There was no gas, much less electricity; we had lamps which had to be cleaned and filled with oil each day, a dirty, troublesome duty. The water for all purposes had to be pumped every morning from a generous well; the idea of a bathroom with hot and cold water, to be got by turning a couple of taps, had never entered anyone's head as a possibility. The only immediate sources of supply of food and other necessaries were a few little shops. My mother's domestic staff was paid in a year about the sum that is demanded each month by such servants as can be obtained to-day by a mistress of immaculate record as an employer. We lived in conditions of self-sufficiency which it is the ambition of modern dictators to achieve, and enjoyed every day as it came.

My father's income was not large, but the Government of the day permitted him to spend almost all of it as he liked, for income tax fell as low as 2d. in the £ (1874–6) and never rose above 6d., when there was a great outcry; the magistrates, who ruled the countryside in quarter sessions, saw to it that the local rates, which they had to pay themselves, were low. It was in many ways an ideal condition of life, free from modern complications and anxieties. I have since been told that though we were comfortable, the working classes had a bad time. My recollection is that they seemed happy and contented, whatever may have been the conditions in the big manufacturing towns and the mining villages. Working for long hours, they brought up large families on a weekly wage which a skilled artisan now receives for a day's labour. Health and unemployment insurance were not even on the political horizon; free education had not been introduced, and old-age pensions were not dreamed of.

In subsequent years the family moved fifteen times, even as far north as Yorkshire. These excursions were made

LADY HURD

SIR EDWARD LAWSON (LORD BURNHAM)

mainly in obedience to the orders of doctors, who thought my father's health would benefit from residence, first, in one place with a sandy soil; then in a town with an open aspect; and then in another for some other reason.

It was owing to one of these migrations that, as a child, I spent a short time in Birmingham, and the family attained lasting fame. My father bought a partnership in that city, and with it a house. He discovered that the house was solid enough, but that the income to be derived from the partnership left a great deal to be desired. So he brought an action against his new partner. He lost it on some technicality to do with contributory negligence, for he had accepted statements without checking them. But he won it in the Court of Appeal. By that time the other party to the action had become a bankrupt. The issue raised a new point of law, and I believe every aspiring solicitor has since had to make himself familiar with the case of *Hurd* v. *Redgrave* before sitting for his final examination.

The sequel to this worrying and costly business was that the family settled in London, without friends so far as I can recall. My father had his plate put up at the entrance to offices in Cheapside, which rocked on Lord Mayor's Day when the bells of Bow Church were rung. It was a daring step to be taken by a man who had hitherto practised in provincial towns and villages, but, as it seems to me, by a miracle he established a flourishing business, to which my brother Martin subsequently succeeded, making it even more flourishing.

In these changing conditions my five brothers and myself grew up. In due course, I entered on the stage of the work-a-day world, hoping to find some rôle suited to such talents as I possessed.

When I look back over the years since I left my home to seek fortune, or as seemed more likely, suffer misfortune, I realise how much I owe to my three successive editors. First I recall E. A. Judges; when I first knew him as the

2

friend of my elder brother Percy,[1] he was the London correspondent of the *Toronto Globe*. Next I passed under the influence of Albert Groser, who *was* the *Western Morning News*, then, although published in Plymouth, a national journal as daily papers were regarded in those days. Then John M. Le Sage, the mainspring of the *Daily Telegraph*, powerfully influenced my life during the later years of the reign in Peterborough Court of Sir Edward Lawson, the managing proprietor of the *Daily Telegraph*. When Sir Edward became Lord Burnham,[2] in 1903, Lord Salisbury, it is said, suggested that it was undesirable that a peer should run a newspaper. Old ideas die; no such veto would be placed on a new peer to-day. His son, Harry Lawson, took charge of the *Daily Telegraph*—the phrase is appropriate to the change in conditions that occurred, for he determined to have more of a say in the affairs of the paper than his father, with advancing years, had had, and he became my mentor. He was jokingly described as "the Honorary Harry" to differentiate him from "the Useful Harry," an amiable Cockney who had charge of the library of the *Daily Telegraph* and was invaluable for facts and figures as they were needed.

Why I became a journalist has often puzzled me. My father, being a solicitor with six sons to start in life, thought the easiest course was to pass them all through his own office, and then leave them to sink or swim in the world. But my brother Percy had had other ideas. He had become secretary to Ernest Rice, of the Besant and Rice partnership in the writing of novels, which in their day had a wide circulation. When Ernest Rice died, my brother joined the staff of the *Staffordshire Sentinel*, and eventually returned to London as the editor of the *Canadian Gazette*. All that I heard of his work fascinated me, and as he shared an office near St. Bride's Church in Fleet Street with E. A.

---

[1] Sir Percy Hurd, M.P. first for Frome 1918–23 and then for Devizes from 1924 onwards.

[2] Lord Burnham died in 1916.

Judges, it was arranged that I should try my hand at newspaper work. It was not at first inspiring, but youth does not look ahead. I clipped from newspapers, "ran messages," and was, I hope, generally useful.

Events gave me my next step. Judges took over the editorship of the *Surrey Times,* of which he had become part-owner. He told me that it would be well if I moved to Guildford, in order to learn something of weekly journalism. So I became a junior reporter on the *Surrey Times.* For two happy years I remained on the staff of that paper, and incidentally, formed a friendship with David Williamson that has never been severed, for I still write for the "Daily Mail Year Book" which he now edits. He was then the assistant editor of the *Sketch,* of which Clement Shorter, whom I had known as a boy, was the editor.

I sometimes wonder whether any youngster ever had an editor who exercised so powerful an influence over his life as Judges exerted over mine. He was my employer in the office and my companion out of it. Strict as to a stranger in the office, exacting the best work I could do—he fathered me in my leisure hours. Each week he set me a book to read and encouraged me to write a review of it, which he read and criticised at the week-end, usually on Friday night when I visited him in his rooms. He was a bachelor at that time, and had few distractions from his ambition to make a success of the *Surrey Times,* though he still spent two or three days at the *Toronto Globe* office in London. Thus he became my father confessor in everything touching my hopes in journalism. On Sundays he took me for long walks, giving me the benefit of his experience in politics and journalism. A man of the highest principle and great industry, he did more than anyone to mould my life.

At this period, Mr. T. B. Potter, a stout-hearted Liberal who was Cobden's successor in the representation of Rochdale, came into my life. It was my duty as a reporter to visit certain towns and villages where the *Surrey Times* had correspondents, and learn from them what had hap-

pened. One summer day I went to the White Hart Hotel
in Haslemere for tea, as I frequently did. I found there an
elderly gentleman with a charming lady, who, I afterwards
learnt, was his second wife. As a result of that chance
meeting, Mr. Potter took me under his wing, sent me the
publications of the Cobden Club, of which he was chairman, and when there was likely to be an interesting debate
in the House of Commons, obtained for me tickets "under
the gallery," seats usually reserved for the private secre-
taries of Ministers and civil servants. Thus I came to hear
some of the great Parliamentary speakers of the day, including Gladstone. I can still recall Mr. Potter's enthusiasm
for the liberalising movement, education being in the fore-
front of it. Since then the education net has been spread
much wider, the expenditure on the schools has reached
dizzy heights, and a generation has grown up which looks
to the taxpayer as the goose that lays the golden egg. The
general level of comfort and happiness has been enormously
raised, and that is to be set on one side of the balance-
sheet. But is the present generation better equipped to use
its mind and its hands than was the last generation?

Judges had repeatedly advised me not to remain too long
on a weekly journal, but to seek experience on a provincial
daily newspaper. When I was recovering at home from a
long illness which had severed, for the time, my association
with the *Surrey Times,* chance led to my obtaining an introduction to Albert Groser, whose London relations I had
known in a casual way for some years. I have never forgotten being asked to tea at the house of his cousin, William
Groser, in Crouch End, in order to meet the editor of the
Western Morning News. William Groser was a man of
humility which I have never known excelled by anyone
else of such high ability. He was a scholar, being a B.Sc.
of London University, and for many years he acted as the
superintendent of the Sunday school at Park Chapel,
Crouch End, which during the ministry of Dr. Alfred
Rowland rivalled the City Temple under Dr. Joseph Parker.

Every weekday he went to the City to carry on the old family business of gold assayer. I went to tea as arranged, met Albert Groser, and also his daughter, whom I forthwith decided to marry, if she would consent. We were married on September 18th, 1895, after Albert Groser had died in Egypt after a long illness.

Why do women marry journalists if they have the chance of linking their lives with a butcher, baker, candlestick-maker or any man who lives a regular life with a more or less assured income? After nearly fifty years I have not answered that question to my own satisfaction. For a journalist is the sport of events. He has no regular hours for meals, so the home is difficult to manage, especially if there are children with school hours to be strictly observed. He is here, there and everywhere in accordance with the orders of his editor. If he is a leader writer on a daily paper, he must be away from home every evening through-out the year except Saturday—for papers were published on Good Fridays and Christmas Days until recent years. His wife is thus cut off from practically all social life. She can never, except on one evening a week, go out to dinner or to the theatre with him. Even his holidays are liable to be interrupted if something unexpected happens as, in my experience, it frequently did!

The life of a country doctor's wife is somewhat of a "mixed grill," her husband being at the beck and call of his patients day and night. But the palm of martyrdom I should give to the journalist's wife, especially as in years gone by the profession was regarded by many people as parasitical. It was not to be classed with any of the learned professions, the Church, the law or medicine. A young man just became a journalist. If he rose to be an editor, he acquired a certain standing, but if he were known simply as on the staff of the *Daily* —— his wife counted for little or nothing. She had to make her own social life with little or no assistance from her husband, who, when she was longing to go to a theatre or accept

an evening engagement, would be toiling and moiling at
his work.

I was gaining wide general experience in daily journalism
on the *Western Morning News* when Albert Groser changed
what seemed likely to be the course of my life. I had rooms
near his house, and sometimes I walked home with him in
the early hours of the morning. On one of these occasions
he told me that the retired naval officer who was editing
the *Naval and Military Record* had asked to be relieved
immediately, as he was going to London to try his hand
at writing plays. No successor was available, and I should
have to take charge of this paper. It had not existed for
more than a few years. It was the child of the *Western
Morning News*, which had always given more news of the
Royal Navy than any other daily paper, and gained fame
for its early information of promotions and appointments.
Wherever men-of-war went, the *Western Morning News*
was despatched to some subscriber. It was decided to
reprint all this naval information, with some additional
articles, in a weekly journal. In this way what came to
be known affectionately in the Royal Navy, without reflection, as I believe, on its accuracy, as the *Dockyard Liar*,
entered upon its long career.

I was twenty-two years of age when I was told that I had
to take charge of this paper until a new editor could be
found. I pointed out that I knew nothing of naval affairs.
My interest hitherto had been in the development of the
holiday resorts of the West Country, and in prevailing on
the local authorities to take advantage of the new Act of
Parliament which permitted them to insist on the notifica-
tion of infectious disease which was periodically the scourge
of ill-drained villages, with water supplies not above suspicion. These and kindred subjects interested me deeply.
My only concern with the sea had been while assisting in
collecting information on coast communications for a series
of articles which "A. G." had arranged to contribute to
The Times. Incidentally, these articles were effective in

persuading the Government of the day to connect coastguard
and lifeboat stations, and also the lighthouses, by telephone.
Thousands of lives were thus saved from the sea.

Albert Groser listened patiently to my mildly expressed
objections to the new work.   But as he entered his house,
he explained that he still thought I could carry on for the
time, and that he would find a new editor as soon as
possible so that I might return to the work I was doing.
I put my back into my new task.   Month succeeded month.
The long-sought-for naval officer did not appear.   Afterwards I was given, in addition to the *Naval and Military
Record,* the conduct of the *Western Weekly News*—so as
to keep me from idling, as "A. G." explained.

Albert Groser was qualified to play a part on a bigger
stage than Plymouth could provide.   He had a greater
interest in national than in local affairs.   He was one of
the best-known provincial journalists in political circles in
London, though he lived and worked in Devonshire; he
often attended important political gatherings in London as
well as the receptions which were held from time to time
at the Foreign Office.   But he was pinned down to Plymouth
by a tragedy.

The *Western Morning News* was owned and edited by
Edward Spender, the uncle of Alfred Spender, who for so
many years was editor of the *Westminster Gazette* and the
brilliant interpreter of long-sighted Liberalism.   The
arrangement was that Edward Spender should live in
London, acting as absentee editor, and writing the leaders
and the London Letter, the latter a feature which he had
introduced into journalism, and that Groser should act as
editor in Plymouth.   Spender and his family were frequent
visitors to Devonshire.   One day Albert Groser was stunned
by the news that the father and two of his sons, while
bathing at Whitsand Bay on the Cornish border, had been
drowned.   This meant that the acting editor became the
actual editor, but with a board of directors over him.
These were men not above average ability, a doctor and a

solicitor among them, who represented the family interests.

Owing to this event, Groser found himself chained to Plymouth by loyalty to his old "chief," and the invitation which reached him in later years to become editor of the *Liverpool Daily Post* came too late.   He was, by that time, in effect the *Western Morning News,* though the directors had the power to stifle his enterprise.   Towards the end of his life these amateurs were a source of increasing irritation to "A. G." and the cause of a good deal of amusement to the members of the staff.

After Groser's experiences, I determined that in no circumstances would I have anything to do with a paper controlled by directors.   Better by far the possible injustice of a dictator than the vacillations of men without knowledge of the way to conduct a newspaper, bewildered by their responsibilities and often divided in purpose.   I recall that on one occasion during my later association with the paper, I wrote to the board asking for an increase of salary.   Weeks elapsed and, knowing that I was doing good work in editing the two weekly papers, as well as writing occasional leaders for the *Western Morning News,* I wrote to say that, as I had had no refusal, I assumed that I was to be better paid, and that the increased pay would be retrospective to the date of my letter.   I received no answer.   During those weeks of waiting, the chairman, for whom I had an affection, would occasionally press a cheque for a small sum into my breast pocket, telling me not to be impatient.   The weeks became months, and when at last the directors made up their minds what to do, I received a considerable cheque, on which I married.   But, in order that the other members of the staff might not be encouraged to ask for higher salaries, the increased pay which had been given me came out of a private account.   I was asked not to talk about the generosity with which I had been treated.

My main interest after I had been given charge of the two weekly papers was the *Naval and Military Record,* and I lost no chance of gaining fuller knowledge of things naval. In this way I first became acquainted, by letter, with Captain John Rushworth Jellicoe; he was then acting as Chief-of-Staff to Admiral Sir Edward Seymour, who was in command of the International Naval Brigade, which was suppressing the Boxer Rebellion in China. He wrote asking me to do him a small service, and thus a friendship began which lasted until his death and burial in St. Paul's Cathedral.

In the course of my naval adventures I forced myself—I am afraid there is no other word for my action—on the notice of Admiral the Hon. Sir Edmund Fremantle, Commander-in-Chief at Plymouth. I sought opportunities to call on him. The great-grandson of one of Nelson's captains, he was a fine type of Victorian, a strict disciplinarian, with a grasp of naval affairs which often made him irritable when the private telegraph line from the Sea Lords at the Admiralty in London, or, as he surmised, often only a clerk acting on their authority, instructed him to do something of which he did not approve. One morning I found him fuming in his office at Mount Wise over an order that he had just received. What it was he did not, of course, tell me. He had come to treat me with confidence, and he held forth generally on the sins of the Admiralty. At last he launched an attack on the designs of the cruisers which were being built, to the plans of Sir William White, Director of Naval Construction; he compared them unfavourably with the better armed and swifter vessels which had been designed by Sir Philip Watts and built at the Armstrong Yard on the Tyne for various foreign governments. His criticisms were not based on secret information. His remarks greatly impressed and even alarmed me.

I made further enquiries, and at last, greatly daring, wrote an article which I sent to the *Nineteenth Century*. To my surprise Mr. (afterwards Sir) James Knowles, the editor, wrote stating that, if he were satisfied as to the accuracy of my facts and deductions, he was inclined to publish my article. It was really an attack on Sir William

White, whose word on the design of men-of-war had hitherto been accepted as final. I consulted the Admiral. He was an officer of great independence, and was afraid of no one. He permitted me to reply that the criticisms were based on correct information.

Thus I made my debut as a naval writer. The *Daily Chronicle,* a London morning newspaper, now lost in the triple amalgamations which have produced the *News Chronicle,* devoted a leading article to the subject, and other papers commented upon it. Sir William White was furious that an unknown youngster should have been allowed to condemn his designs. The editor of the *Nineteenth Century* conceded him the right of reply, and in the next issue a long defence was published—but in small type at the end of the issue. Thenceforward I was a frequent contributor of articles on naval topics, and became acquainted personally with Sir James Knowles. I began to write also for the daily and weekly papers. At last I was greatly rejoiced by the *Daily Telegraph* accepting an article.

About this time I was staying at "Huntly," a hydropathic establishment near Teignmouth, and met once more David Williamson, who was then editing the *Windsor Magazine.* He suggested that I should write an article for him. I was very diffident, but he assured me that his readers would be interested in knowing how bluejackets were trained; I could get photographs of the boys on board the training ship *Impregnable,* then moored in the Hamoaze. I promised to submit the article to him, but without much expectation that it would be accepted. The article was published.

This proved to be a turning-point in my career. It was the custom for the latest issues of the magazines to be placed on a table in the room of Mr. (afterwards Sir) John Le Sage, the managing editor of the *Daily Telegraph.* One evening, as he was leaving for dinner, he picked up the *Windsor Magazine,* in which my article appeared with some striking photographs. He glanced through it while dining. On returning to the office, he told the chief sub-editor that it was interesting, and as there was no pressure of news, a column or so was to be quoted.

That incident was to lead to an association of thirty years with the *Daily Telegraph*. A few days later I received a letter offering me a position on the editorial staff. I was making a satisfactory income at Plymouth by my pen. I regretfully explained that I was married, and could not afford to make the sacrifice which acceptance of the invitation would involve. It was a great disappointment, because my desire was to find regular work on the staff of a daily paper in London. A few days later Le Sage wrote again, to say that he had shown my letter to Sir Edward Lawson. In a word, he asked me what I thought I should be paid. The salary I named was not a large one, though higher than had been first mentioned by Le Sage. Thus it came about that in October 1899, when the South African War was opening, I joined the *Daily Telegraph* in the dual capacity of leader writer and naval correspondent.

I recall my first meeting with Le Sage. I was in the waiting-room, feeling very nervous at the thought of the coming interview with the managing editor of such a newspaper, when a fresh-looking, energetic man entered in his shirt-sleeves. In a few minutes he had summed me up, told me it was not necessary for Sir Edward Lawson to see me, had given me instructions as to the date when I should begin my duties, and I was again in Fleet Street, realising that I had the ball at my feet.

My removal from Plymouth meant that I had to reorganise my life. I had so far settled in that pleasant town, which Drake first made for ever famous, that I had built a small house at Yelverton, nine miles away, where my wife and I hoped to spend week-ends. A few months earlier a friend of mine was attending a sale of land on Dartmoor in company with a local builder, and he invited me to go with him. As, on our homeward journey, we passed through what was then the little village of Yelverton, the builder pointed to a spot commanding fine views of the tors, and remarked that one day someone would build a house there—and not be sorry for it. On the spur of the moment I said I would build the house if the land was available. Thus the foundations came to be laid of "Caredon." I told the local bank manager what I was doing. I should be drawing cheques in order to pay the builder, which meant that I should have an overdraft. He agreed without a moment's hesitation. There was no reference to "Head Office", as there would be today. He was really the manager, who knew his clients and acted on his own judgment instead of having to refer every transaction to men knowing nothing of the character of the depositors of the branch.

But, though this little house was built and furnished and my wife, with our little daughter Vivyen, went to live there, I never entered it. After we settled in London, I sold it—and not at a loss.

CHAPTER II

THE OLD AND NEW ORDERS

THE old traditions of journalism were being undermined in the closing years of the nineteenth century. Alfred Harmsworth (afterwards Lord Northcliffe), the founder of *Answers*, had started a daily newspaper on new lines, the *Daily Mail*. It was intended to meet the needs of the generation which had grown up since the introduction of free compulsory education—"people who could read but not think," as a cynic described them.

While still at Plymouth, I had suggested to him that, as he was Parliamentary candidate for Portsmouth, he might back me in starting a naval journal to be published every week from London. He listened to all I had to say; his secretary—afterwards Sir George Sutton—sat in an alcove throughout the interview. At last Harmsworth explained that he was so preoccupied with the plans for the *Daily Mail* that he had no time for anything else. The new naval journal was thus stillborn.

Harmsworth challenged in his new paper everything for which the old-established daily papers stood in the treatment of news as well as editorial comment. The *Daily Mail*, which was sold at one halfpenny, was intensely alive. Its reports of events were shorter; its descriptive articles were vivid; its leaders were brief and very much to the point.

I joined the *Daily Telegraph* when a revolution in journalism was in progress. London had for many years been the best served city in the world so far as full and accurate news and well-considered comment were concerned. Since the first issue of the *Daily Mail* appeared in 1896, many of the old-established papers have disappeared one after another, because their owners failed to adapt them to the new conditions. The *Standard*, the organ of sane Conservatism, succumbed first. The *Morning Post*—sometimes described as "Jeames's Journal," but really an admirably written exponent of die-hard Conservatism—was swallowed by the *Daily Telegraph* a few years ago; the *Pall Mall Gazette*, the *Globe*, the *Daily News*, the *Daily Chronicle*, the *Sun*, the *Morning Leader* and the *Echo*, among daily papers, have all in turn ceased to exist, as well as the *Saturday Review*, the *Athenæum*, the *Outlook* and many others. I do not suggest that Harmsworth was directly responsible for this high rate of mortality, but the reading public demanded changes in their newspapers and Harmsworth was the first to recognise that demand.

At the time when the *Daily Mail* was first published, the "young lions of Peterborough Court," as the staff of the *Daily Telegraph* had been called by Matthew Arnold, were either dead or in retirement. Clement Scott, George Augustus Sala, Thornton Hunt, Geoffrey Prowse, Edward Blanchard, Edward Dicey and others were only names. Sir Edwin Arnold, who had been the editor of the *Daily Telegraph* and was then remembered by his poem "The Light of Asia," was a more recent memory. He still occasionally, though nearly blind, wrote for the paper. I remember seeing him in his brougham at the main door of the *Daily Telegraph* in Fleet Street talking to Le Sage, and being told that he had married a Japanese lady. His son by his first marriage, Lester Arnold, was on the staff in my time.

A new order in journalism was opening. Sir Edward Lawson, the managing proprietor of the *Daily Telegraph*, did not realise the significance of events for some time. He had succeeded his father, Joseph Moses Levy, and had added to the prestige and circulation of the paper, but in "make-up" and in type it was still Victorian. Short in stature, always well dressed, with the silkiest of top hats, Lawson was a notable figure, who knew everyone and was liked by everyone. Though he had always described himself as a Liberal until the Home Rule split, he was conservative in his attitude towards journalism.

But the "young lions" had gone and their places had to be filled. On the advice of Le Sage, additions were made to the staff. Iwan Muller, who had been associated with Harry Cust on the *Pall Mall Gazette*, was one of the first recruits; others, J. L. Garvin, J. B. Firth and Edwin Wilcox, joined the staff about the same time as I did. W. L. Courtney, a typical Oxford don, was then the literary editor, the most cheering and helpful colleague any young journalist could have hoped to have. He was another editor whose name I hold in grateful memory, for he not only advised me on many matters, but permitted me to write frequently for the *Fortnightly Review*, which he edited. He was also chairman of Chapman and Hall, the publishers of Dickens among other famous writers. He appeared rather indolent, but he was, in fact, a hard worker and yet always accessible.

It was a coincidence that on joining the *Daily Telegraph* I met two former colleagues, E. L. Goodman, who had been at Guildford when I was there and was the foreign editor of the paper, and Walter G. Bell, who since then has become a widely read historian of his native London. Bell, even when young, suffered from the handicap that he looked younger than he was. When I was at Plymouth he had been the understudy of Rowe Bennett, the London correspondent of the *Western Morning News*. When his chief was ill, he wrote the leaders as well as the London Letter, and very admirably he did them. But when a successor to Bennett had to be found, Bell was not appointed, because it was considered by the directors, all well on in life, that he was too young. When will old men realise that youth is not a crime to be punished? It is one of the tragedies of the professions and businesses that old men will usurp the places which should be occupied by men with all the initiative and courage of youth. They believe that they themselves are indispensable. That is the most deadly disease of old age. No one is indispensable, as history proves. There are always plenty of pebbles on the beach quite as round and quite as polished as those which the tide carries away. Old age is not a blessing, but a curse. Browning's lines, "Grow old along with me, the best is yet to be," should be regarded as an invitation to the young to draw up alongside us as friends and colleagues in life's tasks so that they may carry on the torch when we can no longer press on in the race, which is to the young and not to the old. The primary duty of old age is to make it easy for younger men to take the helm as soon as they are qualified to do so.

The *Daily Telegraph* was what in the Navy would be described as a "happy ship." We were a band of brothers in the sense in which Nelson used that phrase—brothers under discipline. Many things contributed to these pleasant conditions, but much was due to Sir Edward Lawson [1] and his son and successor, as well as to Le Sage, then mellowing with the passage of years. One day I was instructed to go to the studio in St. John's Wood of Signor Martino, who had been marine painter to Queen Victoria, and to write an article on a series of pictures he had painted depicting the battle of Trafalgar. It was hoped that they would be purchased by the nation. I had an idea that the suggestion came to Lord Burnham from King Edward VII. I knew nothing of the art of painting, but the pictures impressed me. I wrote a column in the *Daily Telegraph,* and Martino was so pleased that he sent me a picture of the *Victory* saluting the first Dreadnought. When I reached the office on the evening after publication, I found a pencilled note which I still treasure. "My dear boy, you have never written anything better than this morning's article.—B." He could be severe, but every member of the staff knew that for good work he would receive a pat on the back. Like father, like son.

[1] Sir Edward Lawson was raised to the peerage as Lord Burnham in 1903.

THE PRINCIPAL MEMBERS OF THE STAFF OF THE "DAILY TELEGRAPH"—1918

Back Row—Mr. H. Meek, Mr. E. T. Williamson, Mr. W. R. Williamson, Mr. Francis Caine, Mr. D. Ross Williams
Middle Row—Mr. C. A. Reeve, Mr. H. C. Bailey, Mr. T. B. Firth, Mr. E. C. Bentley, Mr. Fred Miller, Mr. J. Hall Richardson.
Mr. John Martin, Mr. Sidney Galtrey, Mr. Southey, Mr. Frank Hare, The Hon. Harry Lawson.
Front Row—Mr. Bennet Burleigh, Mr. John M. Le Sage, LORD BURNHAM, Mr. W. L. Courtney, Sir Claude Phillips
(Sir Archibald Hurd was ill and unable to attend this gathering at Hall Barn)

In later years I came to appreciate the character of his son, who became managing proprietor. The second Lord Burnham was the ideal "chief"—kind, appreciative, sympathetic. He was immersed in public work, but regular in his attendance at the office in the morning and again at night, after he had fulfilled one of his many engagements. I think he was one of those rare men who enjoy speaking in public, and he spoke well. But, in spite of all his activities, he knew everything that was going on in the *Daily Telegraph* office. He was the friend as well as the employer of the staff. When the rush of the night's work was over, he would often come to my room and talk over current events. At heart, he remained a liberal with a small "l"; he was no longer, as he had been when sitting for several years in the House of Commons, a Liberal in the political sense of that word.

Lord Burnham was distinguished by the same common sense as his father had been. He faced facts in the social and political spheres. I have preserved one letter from him which he wrote me during the Great War when Lloyd George was trying to support public confidence by adopting expedients, with reference in particular to shipping, shipbuilding and agriculture, which many people thought unwise. I was staying at Bude at the time:

> THE "DAILY TELEGRAPH,"
> FLEET STREET, LONDON, E.C.4.
> *July 5th, 1917.*

MY DEAR HURD,

Many thanks for your letter and for the enclosure, which I return herewith.

You know that I am in close sympathy and agreement with the views which you hold, and substantially with those expressed in Runciman's letter.[1] Free tonnage is the real need, and all this exaggerated talk about the results of ploughing up grass lands and cultivating the commons diverts attention from the vital issue of shipbuilding.

[1] Later Viscount Runciman of Doxford.

I very much regret that Lloyd George has lent himself even in a slight degree to the bunkum about profiteering, which is doing so much harm among the working classes.

I hope you are feeling the full effect of the good air you so thoroughly deserve.

Yours very truly,

BURNHAM.

Le Sage was the sun round which, as a young member of the staff, I moved when I first joined the *Daily Telegraph*. He was undoubtedly a notable man. When, on a fine morning, he walked with something of a jaunty air between his chambers in Clements Inn, abutting on to the Law Courts, and the *Daily Telegraph* office—eastward in the morning and westward at night—he looked like the colonel of a cavalry regiment who had wandered by mistake into Fleet Street. He was above the average height, erect of bearing, with grey hair and moustache, and a rubicund face—in every way a fine figure of a man. You were tempted to look back at him, wondering what purpose lurked in his steady, fearless gaze, where he was going and what he intended to do. You wondered still more if you caught his smile as he nodded to a friend, for it was a smile with a meaning. How many of the passers-by recognised in this soldierly man the managing editor of the *Daily Telegraph,* who became the doyen of London journalists?

John Merry Le Sage was of all men connected with newspapers whom I have met the most intriguing, to use a much-abused word. He was a born dictator, and he brooked no rivalry in his own sphere. But, in all that he thought, said or did he was the shadow of the three successive managing proprietors of the *Daily Telegraph*—Joseph Moses Levy, Edward Lawson and Harry Lawson, father, son and grandson, over a period of upwards of fifty years. That was his strength as well as theirs. His attachment to them was the dominating loyalty of his life. In his relations with his staff, it was a case of liking or disliking at first sight. If a journalist wanted to join the staff of the *Daily Telegraph* and "J. M. L."—then its master mind—liked the look of him, all was well. He was a "big" man in every way—mentally and physically, but he could be very petty. Subject only to the ruling of his successive masters, he insisted on his own way. While he was in harness, there was only one editor of the *Daily Telegraph*. If Le Sage heard that anyone was describing himself as "sporting editor," or "financial editor," or, in fact, any sort of editor, he put his foot down decisively. He made it clear that there was only one editor, and he was that editor.

Le Sage was a sagacious man, with an indomitable will. He never admitted defeat until the last, when in his eighty-ninth year he passed on. His success in journalism was all the more remarkable because he was in no sense a literary man: he read little except the newspapers, and never to my knowledge put his pen to paper except to sign letters. He had a "nose for news" and an uncanny insight into the meaning of events, and his judgment was seldom wrong. His university was the world, for he was a travelled man. His interests were world politics and national politics. It was said that the *Daily Telegraph* each morning reflected what the man on the knifeboard of the horse-drawn bus was thinking, and that was due to the inspiration of Le Sage. There were depths in him which few men fathomed. He was apparently a simple-minded man. He saw no graduations between black and white. He believed to the end that the people of this country would not tolerate more than two political parties. He never lost faith in the common sense of the British people or in the future of the British Empire, and he believed that the first duty of the British peoples was to command the sea. There was a fascination about his steadfastness of faith that was a tonic to those of less settled convictions.

When Le Sage completed "Fifty Years of Fleet Street" a dinner was given to him by the staff of the *Daily Telegraph*, and the Hon. Harry Lawson, as he then was, presided and paid an eloquent tribute to this old and loyal servant of his family. The preceding fifty years, he remarked, had seen a transformation in things political, things social and things material which "daze the eye and rack the mind."

It is bewildering to think of what has happened. The map of the world has been unrolled and half of it has been repainted. Some part of it has been coloured for the first time at the expense of the *Daily Telegraph*.[1] But it is not only the map of the world which has been treated in that way. The map of life itself has been drawn afresh by the instruments of science and by the novelties of mechanism. Our guest to-night has seen all this, and he has seen it not from the street corner; he has drunk it in at the head centre of daily knowledge and daily experience. For the last half-century Fleet Street has been the main thoroughfare of all that the world has been doing and seeing, and John Le Sage has been there all the time. He has seen the dynasties of the world rise and fall; he has seen some of the dynasties of the Press world rise and fall, but he has not seen them *all* fall. We certainly would not say of him, as was said of Charles Greville, "For fifty years he listened at the door. And heard some secrets, and invented more." There have been few secrets he has not heard, but I well know there are none he ever invented. He would say what we all know to be true: "The British public hates lies, and lies do not pay."

Le Sage's reply to the toast reminded the younger members of the staff of his varied experiences. When he joined the *Daily Telegraph* there was no telegraphing. At the General Election of 1865, when speeches were still being delivered on the hustings and the figures of the poll were declared every half-hour, he was sent to Tiverton to report a speech by Lord Palmerston. He called on that statesman early in the evening. Le Sage was going back to London after the speech had been made. On learning the time of the train, Palmerston said, "Well, have your luggage sent to the station, stand in front of the hustings,

[1] This was a reference to Stanley's exploratory expedition in "Darkest Africa," which the *Daily Telegraph* helped to organise and finance.

and tell me how many minutes I have left, and you will catch your train." Le Sage wrote the speech in the train, and it appeared the following morning. That was not a unique experience. Politicians usually show the utmost consideration to journalists, and the more distinguished the politician, usually the greater the consideration.

Le Sage was the first London editor, I believe, to receive the honour of Knighthood, and the distinction was suitably celebrated at a luncheon. On that occasion he recalled some of his memories. During the Russo-Turkish conflict, it was Le Sage who first gave Lord Derby the startling intelligence that Disraeli had ordered the British Fleet to the Dardanelles, an event which affected the whole course of foreign policy. Lord Derby, who was Secretary of State for Foreign Affairs, knew nothing about the movement. Le Sage entered Paris with the Germans, staying afterwards in the city. He braved the terrors of the Commune, interviewing its leaders in "their den." Moreover, he saw Gladstone come to the office of the *Daily Telegraph* and try to make his peace with the paper after the Balkan atrocities. Later he saw Parnell and Davitt arrive to explain the meaning of their land policy and the justification for Home Rule.

Among letters which I treasure is the last characteristic reply from Le Sage to a message of good cheer which I sent him after his retirement from the *Daily Telegraph*:

SAN REMO, BELGRAVE ROAD,
TORQUAY.
Christmas Day, 1923.

MY DEAR HURD,
Many thanks for your letter. All my best congratulations and good wishes for "The Day" and continued success for the Coming Year.
Your clear duty is to save the British Navy from the spoilers of any political party.
What a Political situation! *Ultimately*, Asquith won't win fame by voting with the Reds to defeat the Govern-

ment. He ought—in my opinion—to support the Government and then later on form, perhaps, some sort of National party to keep out our common foe.

In the hotel—it really isn't one—there is an old Pekinese —called Togo! But he is not an Admiral—I believe he comes from Manchester. His owner is a Portuguese!

Ever,

Myself   JOHN M. LE SAGE.

Not at all well—

No appetite.

ARCHIBALD HURD, ESQR.

The thirty years that I spent with the *Daily Telegraph* were almost uniformly happy. The most memorable times were late at night when we had done our writing. Gradually into the library, the great central hall with its gallery and bookshelves, one after another of us would drift to await proofs from the printing room. Conversation would become general. Iwan Muller, who was a friend of Balfour, George Wyndham and many political figures of the day, was full of anecdotes. Garvin, however, usually dominated these evenings. Germany was on the horizon as a possible enemy. Garvin was more familiar with German history and literature than anyone I have ever met. At that time he was a voracious reader, even when at his meals. He was as brilliant a talker as he was a writer, and he held us all as by a spell. Once when my wife and I came across him in an hotel at Ryde, he sat with us in the garden and before we realised the passage of time a neighbouring clock struck 1 a.m.!

On the eve of the Great War, E. C. Bentley crossed Fleet Street from the *Daily News* to join us. He was a welcome recruit to our little company, for he combined the preciseness of the lawyer—he had been called to the Bar on coming down from Oxford—with a charming literary style. While I wrote rapidly, and no doubt often carelessly, Bentley would not be hurried, however urgent the call for "copy." He never wrote a slovenly sentence, nor did he ever pass into the frenzy which would seize Garvin when he was dealing with a subject on which he felt deeply. Bentley will perhaps be longest remembered as the author of what, I believe, is the best of detective stories, "Trent's Last Case," but his finest work is buried in the files of the *Daily Telegraph*.

These midnight seances would sometimes be joined by Malcolm Watson, the dramatic critic, and by Lionel Monckton, adored by frequenters of the Gaiety Theatre for his delightful music. Nor can I forget the calm indifference to the talk that went on around him of Edward Goodman, the censor of the leaders, and the father of my friend, E. L. Goodman. He was then an old man, who no doubt regarded us all as mere boys. As he read proofs amid the swift passage of argument, he preserved a surprising patience, going on with his task as though we did not exist. He was a neighbour of mine at Hampstead, and many a time, when for some reason the horse-drawn tram to Hampstead was not running, he and I would walk home and he would tell me of the old days of the Savage Club, of which he was honorary secretary for many years.

From time to time Robin Legge, the musical critic, would come in from a concert. He was on *The Times* when I joined the *Daily Telegraph,* and was elected to the Savile Club. One afternoon, as I was playing billiards, I asked him if he had heard that Joseph Bennett, who had done the musical criticism on the *Daily Telegraph* for many years, was retiring. He said that he would like to fill the vacancy, and at once left the club. A few days later I heard from him that he had immediately applied for the post, with success. He was the friendliest member of the Savile in those days, always coming forward to make a newcomer welcome to the friendliest club of which I have ever had experience, with Charles Villiers Stanford, Edward Elgar, Ray Lancaster, Gervase Elwes, Harry Plunket Greene, Alan Barlow, Henry Higgs among its outstanding members.

In my days, the writing of leaders was usually not finished before ten or eleven at night. I would then wait to see a proof in order to check any statement of fact or vary an opinion in accordance with the latest news. How many times have I reached home in broad daylight, with body worn out and nerves in a jangle! I recall one experience. The incident occurred on a winter morning about two o'clock. I was then living at Hampstead and no tram was available. After dismissing the horse-drawn Hansom cab at the bottom of the hill—for the drivers usually refused to go farther than Hampstead Heath station—I was walking by the side of the desolate heath, mysterious in the darkness. I heard footsteps behind me. I increased my pace. The footsteps came nearer. Then I raced up the hill and at last reached my home in Christchurch Road, wondering what lunatic or criminal had been pursuing me.

I had never forgotten the experience of a colleague at Plymouth. In the early hours of the morning he was stopped by a man who exclaimed "Ticket, please" in a hortatory voice. My friend realised that he had to deal with a madman. Fortunately, he had two tram tickets in his pocket, and he instantly handed them over. The man said he would see if they were all right and moved towards a lamp-post. My friend took to his heels. He learnt afterwards that a railway ticket collector, with dangerous tendencies if thwarted, had escaped from an asylum. With this experience in my mind, I was glad to close the door of my home, leaving, as I thought, the lunatic or criminal to his own devices. The next night when I reached the office, a colleague, S. J. Glanville, who also lived at Hampstead, said, "I tried to overtake you last night, but you pelted up the hill like mad. I should have called to you, but I was not quite sure if it was you." I assured him that his surmise was correct, and told him the story of the madman to explain my haste in seeking the shelter of my home.

No railway trains were available for the night workers in Fleet Street who lived in the north-western suburbs. They had to rely on horse-drawn trams. It was a very slow mode of travel, and desperately cold in the winter for those of us who preferred to sit on the exposed seats on the top. Many a morning we reached our homes frozen to the bone, but these experiences apparently did us no harm. One of my frequent companions was that modern Gallahad, H. W. Nevinson, the friend of every unpopular cause that appealed to his generous soul. He was then a leader writer on one of the Liberal daily papers, but whenever a war broke out he was restless until he could pack his things and get into the midst of the fighting as correspondent for a newspaper. And yet he was the most peaceful of men. Another companion of those wearisome tram journeys was Vaughan Nash, who was a leader writer by night and private secretary to Asquith by day. He was a man, like Nevinson, of lofty ideals, who believed that Liberalism offered a remedy for many, if not most, of the social evils of the world. He was not a great talker, but when he discussed any problem of the day he was always worth listening to, for he spoke from a wide knowledge and with a keen, if quietly expressed, sympathy.

How full of confidence in ourselves we were! How assured we were of the rightness of the opinions expressed in the *Daily Telegraph*. How seriously we took ourselves. I have since glanced over a number of cuttings of leaders I wrote. What a variety of subjects! Though naval and shipping matters were the topics which I preferred, I had to deal with many other subjects. There was one leader of one and three-quarter columns on the mission of nurses which Le Sage refused to have reduced in length! One afternoon when the Derby had been run under notable circumstances, Le Sage told me that that would be the subject of my leader. I explained that I had never seen a horse-race, and knew little more about the Derby than that it was run at Epsom, and so on. He clinched the matter by saying that I should come to the subject with all the more freshness in that it was so new to me. But that leading article did not lead anyone anywhere.

Usually the subjects of the leaders were discussed in Le Sage's room late in the afternoon. He would sit toying with a letter opener or a pencil as he held forth on one topic after another in general terms, leaving the writer to develop the ideas which he threw out. But sometimes, he would be more specific, as on an occasion when he sent me instructions by express messenger.

Before giving these, I must explain that during the Russo-Japanese War I had written practically each day in the *Daily Telegraph* on the course of naval events in the Far East. It was customary for Admiral James Ingles, who had been adviser to the Japanese Admiralty in the early days of that country's naval development, to come to the office each evening to discuss matters with me. Le Sage was greatly impressed by the manner in which Admiral Togo handled his fleet at the Battle of Toushima. He forthwith christened me "Togo," and by that name I was known to him in later years—unless he was displeased with something I had done.

THE "DAILY TELEGRAPH,"
FLEET STREET, LONDON, E.C.
September 25th, 1913.

DEAR TOGO,
          As you have a well-balanced mind, partly religious, partly civil, and understand thoroughly the responsibilities of marriage, I think you might write us an interesting descriptive kind of leader on the facts published about the increase of civil marriages. I do not want any moral drawn, or any conclusion either in favour of the Church or in favour of civil marriages; but it is clear from statistics that there are many more civil marriages than there were a few years ago.

I won't say what class of society is content to be married before a registrar instead of in the Church. Undoubtedly one reason is that a great number of people do not want the bother and fuss and trouble involved in a marriage at church, and they are, therefore, content with the simple rite at the registrar's office, which, from the legal point of view, is just as good.

I should think there are two reasons why civil marriages have increased; a great number of people do not like the publicity attending the kind of limelight effect of being married in church, and, secondly, of course, there is a very great difference in the cost. If the young people have only limited means, instead of squandering money on dresses and ceremony, they can spend it perhaps in a pleasant trip, etc., etc. Of course, the Church does not like it, but there it is.

I should say that you could not do better than consult your wife; in a matter like this probably she will direct you properly. I enclose a cutting from the *Graphic*.

Of course, the Roman Catholics regard marriage as a Sacrament. In France you have to be married by the civil power as well as by the Church—but that is another thing altogether. The Church of England teaches that it is a very important obligation (to put it mildly) into which you enter. In regard to Nonconformists, I do not think they trouble very much; but in the olden days there was a kind of ecclesiastical terror—lots of young women would have thought that they were not married at all if they were not married by a parson. Being married by a registrar must be a little dull—I should think a little cold. Still, if young people are very much in love with each other probably that would not affect them.

I am old-fashioned enough to think that if I had to be married again, which is not possible, I should still like to go to church, although I am not much of a churchman. The same with children being christened; and when it comes to the last ceremony of all, being buried, people somehow like the religious service. Then the vast majority of people think and feel that the final tribute to the dead would be somewhat wanting in respect and affection if the clergyman or minister did not take part in the last service.

Yours always,

JOHN M. LE SAGE,
Managing Editor.

I was glad that I had not to deal with party politics. I had been nurtured in my father's time on the *Daily News,* and though I always voted Conservative in later years, fearing that progress might be too fast, I talked a good deal of Liberalism. But the clash of party politics did not interest me. Moreover, in the spare time when my work on the *Daily Telegraph* was not onerous, I acted for some years as political secretary to the Earl of Dunraven. Having given up all thought of winning the America's Cup, he was devoting himself to what was known as Devolution, the half-way house to Irish Home Rule. I believed thoroughly in the cause which he pleaded in a series of books in which we collaborated—"The Outlook in Ireland," "The Finances of Ireland," and others. I found the facts, wrote the chapters in draft, and then the particular book gradually took shape as we went through the MS. As published, these volumes were legitimately described as by Lord Dunraven.

It was a tragic business that Balfour deserted George Wyndham, his former Parliamentary Secretary, after, as was said at the time, encouraging him. Wyndham, who had gone to Phœnix Park as Irish Secretary, opened up communications with the moderate Irish leaders. Foundations of Anglo-Irish friendship were being laid, and if such a form of government as Wyndham and Dunraven and a group of influential Irishmen supported had been set up, the subsequent history of Ireland might have been very different. George Wyndham's death was hastened, it was said, by the disappointment of his hopes. He seemed at one time destined to become Prime Minister. I had heard much of him, his ability and charm of manner, when he became part owner of the *Outlook,* which my brother Percy edited for some years. I wrote for it from time to time.

Though my years on the *Daily Telegraph* were almost unclouded, one incident remains in my memory which gave me much anxiety. It arose out of my first meeting with Mr. Winston Churchill. Soon after he became First Lord of the Admiralty in 1911, I received a telephone message from the private secretary to successive First Lords, Mr. (afterwards Sir) James Masterton-Smith, a friend of long standing. He was a man of acute intellect and sound judgment. He asked me to call at the Admiralty, but did not state the purpose of the summons. On my arrival, he told me that the First Lord was waiting to see me. When I entered the room, which had always been occupied by the First Lord, what first attracted me was not the First Lord himself, but a statuette of Nelson which stood on his desk —an innovation. He immediately explained that the Controller of the Navy, whom I knew slightly as a zealous but old-fashioned officer, had complained that I had revealed in the *Daily Telegraph* what he regarded as secrets in connection with the armament of the battleships of the *Royal Sovereign* type which were then building.

War with Germany was at least a possibility, and everyone was rather nervy at the Admiralty. It was not known what surprise the Germans might have for us. The Controller of the Navy was anxious, quite rightly, to guard his own surprises. When he entered the room, this officer told me that I had let out the secret of the armament of the battleships which were then building.

Information as to the decision to mount 13·5 in. guns had, however, already appeared in the *Western Morning News*—a paper read by every naval attaché in London— on the previous Thursday. Apparently, the information was known at Plymouth, where one of the ships was completing for sea. Information as to the mounting of 6 in. guns in barbettes had been *widely* known for some time past, and had been given in the "Daily Mail Year Book," which must have gone to press several weeks earlier. The vessels embodying the design had been under construction at Portsmouth, Devonport, Newcastle-on-Tyne, the Clyde and Birkenhead for nearly a year; variations on that design had been circulated among Powers requiring new ships for months past; a new Brazilian ship building at Elswick, it was known, was to have a more powerful gun than any then mounted in a British battleship; and it would have been surprising if foreign powers had not assumed that since we were building an Argentine vessel in a private yard, as well as a Turkish vessel, with guns firing a 1,400 lb.

shell, the Admiralty were arming British vessels with guns
at least as powerful.

In view of the long interval since the British vessels were
designed, those designs having become known to a large
number of persons employed in Government and private
yards, the Admiralty were to be congratulated on the length
of time that the secret had been kept. The British naval
authorities had thereby gained a very notable lead, since
this country, it was evident, would have six ships with an
older 13·5 in. gun and ten with a new 13·5 in. gun completed and at sea in the spring of 1914, at a moment when
no other first-class naval power would have a more powerful
weapon than the 12 in. gun actually in its fleet.

When the Controller reproached me with the publication
of the armament of these battleships, I replied, "But that
is no secret." He persisted that it was. Turning to the
First Lord, I asked him if there was a "Daily Mail Year
Book" in the Admiralty. When it was brought in, I turned
to the article on the British Navy, and there was a descrip-
tion of the *Royal Sovereign* class with the revelation of the
armament. The First Lord looked at the book, smiled,
and remarked, "I do not think there is anything more to
be said, Admiral." So the Controller left the room.

Then the First Lord began to talk about the work he
was doing for the Navy in order to prepare it for war, if
war should come. We had been talking for several minutes,
when I mentioned one particular matter which had come
to my knowledge. Immediately he turned on me, in what
I was afterwards to realise was his characteristic impulsive
manner, "Who told you that?" I parried the question, but
he persisted in demanding that I should reveal the source
of my information. The incident lasted about half an hour.
He told me that the fact was known only to three persons,
the Prime Minister, Lord Fisher and himself. I assured
him that I had heard it neither from Mr. Asquith nor the
First Sea Lord. This disclosure made him even more persistent in his demand for the name, but as persistently I

refused to give it, though he promised that my informant should in no way suffer.

Throughout this time he continued to walk up and down the room. At last he stood still, and said that it was useless to continue talking. He hoped I would think the matter over and, accepting his pledge, would write and tell him who my informant had been. So we parted. I consulted Mr. Lawson, and he agreed that I could not do other than I had done. I wrote the following letters to Mr. Churchill:

5, DOWNSHIRE HILL,
HAMPSTEAD, N.W.
December 5th, 1911.

DEAR MR. CHURCHILL,

I am exceedingly sorry that my first—and last—visit to the Admiralty since your accession to office should have been so unfortunate. I have been interested in naval affairs for twenty years and this is my first experience of any unpleasantness.

I should have liked to have complied with your request, but on a matter of principle, I cannot give way. You yourself would think very lightly of my discretion and trust-worthiness, I am convinced, if I acted otherwise. The matter was, I believe, mere gossip, and as such I did not publish it. If it was not, then it came to me by third, fourth or fifth hand, and I cannot join in an inquisition. You have told me that the possible purpose was known to only three persons. Which of those had spoken of your purpose—if any of them—I do not know. All I can do is to repeat—as I told Mr. Lawson—that the person is not at the Admiralty.

Yours faithfully,

ARCHIBALD HURD.

5, DOWNSHIRE HILL,
HAMPSTEAD, N.W.
December 5th, 1911.

DEAR MR. CHURCHILL,

One point I omitted to mention in my letter. You told me that you thought of appointing an officer to whom journalists could go. If you carry out this intention, I will undertake always to confer with him before I publish anything, even if it be merely surmise based on deduction, which can conflict with what you consider national interests. I think anyone who knows me will acquit me of having ever consciously put my keenness as a journalist before my duty as an Englishman. I quite appreciate your heavy responsibility at this juncture, and I will certainly do nothing to render it heavier.

Believe me,

Yours faithfully,

ARCHIBALD HURD.

I heard nothing more of the matter. But the sequel shows the sporting character of the First Lord. Some time later the Fleet had been assembled at Portland, and I was staying at the Gloucester Hotel at Weymouth. I may have mentioned to Masterton-Smith before leaving London that that would be my address. At any rate, one morning when I returned to the hotel, I found a message from the First Lord asking me to lunch on board the *Enchantress* the following day. Of course, I accepted the invitation. No word was said of our little contretemps. One incident fixed the day in my memory. I had an afternoon engagement which I mentioned to the First Lord. He immediately spoke across the table to his Naval Secretary, Captain David Beatty, "Call a boat for Mr. Hurd." Beatty was then little known to the public, although everyone in the Service knew that he had distinguished himself in Egypt during the Kitchener campaign. In fact, he had risen in rank so rapidly that he had not been able to put in the necessary sea time for employment as a flag officer. Had he not been chosen by the First Lord as his Naval Secretary and then given the command of a battle-cruiser squadron, he would have gone on the retired list in due course. The boat was called, and I left the *Enchantress* with a new appreciation of the First Lord.

I saw him from time to time later, and well remember

when he left the Admiralty in 1915. He moved at once to a house in Cromwell Road, and I called upon him on the following morning. I found him smoking the inevitable after-breakfast cigar and playing with a meccano set of his son Randolph. "Well, here I am out of office. I thought I was doing fairly well. But I was evidently wrong." I could sympathise with his feelings, because he had brought to the Admiralty the driving force which had been needed at the moment. I recall that about a quarter of an hour later, Sir F. E. Smith, the fallen First Lord's close friend, came into the room, and the three of us studied the large painting which Mr. Churchill, who had recently taken up painting as a hobby, had just completed.

The meeting with the future Lord Chancellor was another interesting incident. I never knew him well, but we had exchanged letters in circumstances which worried me at the time. During the war, when he was Attorney-General, he acted as Chief Censor, and I was told that he had made remarks reflecting on me in the Lobby of the House of Commons. This came to my knowledge in a letter from the Parliamentary correspondent of the *Daily Telegraph*.

Sunday.

DEAR MR. HURD,
I casually mentioned the following to Mr. Le Sage this morning, and he desired me to communicate it to you:

Last Thursday the Attorney-General told me (Martin) that he had had seriously to consider whether he should not institute a prosecution against you under the Defence of the Realm Act with respect to your article in Tuesday's paper on an offensive policy at sea, and that it was only the splendid conduct of the *Daily Telegraph* during the war that had saved the situation.

I told Sir Frederick Smith that I had read the article, and did not think it was at all calculated to give away secrets to the enemy. But he replied that that very policy is under the consideration of the Admiralty at the present

4

time, and he was certain "that if he had proceeded he would have obtained a conviction."

Mr. Le Sage thought that you would like to know this.

Yours ever,
JOHN MARTIN.

I wrote to the Chief Censor asking for details. I was very friendly with the Chief Naval Censor, Admiral Sir Douglas Brownrigg, a seaman of the old school with a hard head, sound judgment and a flow of rich naval language—he was beloved by everyone. He had made no complaint, so I wondered on what authority his chief had spoken. I received no reply to my letter, and I learnt that the Chief Censor had stated that he did not intend to notice my letter. So I then informed him that if he did not withdraw the statement which was damaging to my reputation, I should take legal proceedings to get redress. Perhaps I was too touchy. At any rate, the incident closed with a kindly letter.

August 13th, 1917.

DEAR MR. HURD,

Your article was officially brought before me with the information that a committee was at this moment considering and had not reported upon some of the matters dealt with in your article. I was not even informed that your article (as Mr. Martin now tells me was the case) had been submitted to the Naval Censor. I naturally drew the inference that the article had not been approved, and as an old admirer and reader of the *Telegraph* and (if I may say so) of your own articles, had the conversation referred to (with substantial though not complete accuracy) in this letter from Mr. Martin, who is a Press friend of mine of eleven years' standing. It is quite evident that on the assumption, which I accept, that the Naval Censor had passed your article, it should never have been put before me at all.

My opinion upon it was without foundation, being based upon a natural but erroneous inference.

I have directed immediate enquiries to be made in my department to explain the lack of co-ordination between them and the Admiralty, and the circumstances under which the matter was brought before me at all.

Yours,

FREDERICK SMITH.

While this business was worrying me a good deal I received this letter from Le Sage.

THE "DAILY TELEGRAPH,"
FLEET STREET, LONDON, E.C.4.

August 19th, 1917.

MY DEAR HURD,

I hear that you are not to be tried by court-martial, or at the Old Bailey.

I never did think much of your correspondent, and I think still less of him now. Men who hold that important position have no right to express an opinion, especially one conveying a serious threat, without taking care that they know the facts. It will not affect the stability or the reputation of the journal with which we are both associated.

Yours always,

JOHN M. LE SAGE,

Managing Editor.

I met "F. E." for the first time after this incident on that morning in Cromwell Road. Like his friend, he was a sportsman. He was friendly and cordial, and "the storm in a teacup" was never mentioned by either of us afterwards.

His remarkable intellect brought him high office in later years. I met him for the last time when he had become Lord Birkenhead and had resigned his office as Secretary of State for India. Commander Sir Edward Nicholl, M.P., a Welsh shipowner who had begun life before the mast in the Merchant Navy, decided to give a dinner for "F. E." at the Carlton Club on his retirement from the India Office. He invited me to be one of his guests. It was an evening that I shall never forget. When "F. E." came in he had a slight stoop, as though he had been tired for many days.

As he shook hands with me, I noticed that he had jewelled studs in his shirt and jewelled sleeve-links, and I thought of Disraeli as he had been depicted in my boyhood. When his health had been drunk, in a manner which showed how much his friends admired him, he made a remarkable speech.

It was without reserve. He explained that, when he retired from the Bar, he had saved £70,000, which he thought justified him in devoting his time to national affairs. That belief was not disturbed until he became Secretary of State for India. He came to the conclusion that that office involved the costly entertainment of native princes and others, if he was to maintain, in the national interests, the prestige of the Secretary of State. That hospitality had drained his resources. At last he was forced to the conclusion that he owed a debt to his wife and family, and that he could not sacrifice all their interests to the service of his country and India. So he had decided that he must make another fortune by going into the City. It was a sad speech, and none who heard it will forget the picture of quiet dignity which "F. E." presented that evening as he explained that in some circumstances, national interests, even by a devoted servant of State, must be subordinated to private interests. He had probably the finest intellect of anyone of his day, and as I left the Carlton I reflected that high office ought not to involve such a man in so hard a choice.

It became the practice of the Admiralty towards the latter end of the nineteenth century to hold naval manœuvres each summer, when the Reserve Fleet was mobilised. The available forces were divided, and they engaged in strategical exercises. The principal daily papers, London and provincial, were invited to send representatives on board selected ships. At that time there were many journalists who had made a study of naval affairs. James Thursfield—afterwards Sir James—a former Oxford don and a leader writer in *The Times*, was the most notable of them; Charles Robinson, who had served in the Royal Navy and retired as commander, was that journal's naval correspondent. The *Standard* had on its staff a student in John Leyland, Cope Cornford wrote in the *Morning Post* on naval matters, H. W. Wilson in the *Daily Mail* and Swinburne in the *Daily News*. Each year we went afloat for a fortnight or three weeks, and thus, as the Admiralty no doubt intended, we got to know the ways of the Navy. Owing to the position of the *Daily Telegraph*, I was usually assigned to one of the flagships. Admirals and captains in a flagship chose as a rule young officers of promise. Thus in these cruises I got to know Captain Charles Madden,[1] Captain (later Admiral of the Fleet Sir) Henry Oliver, Lieutenant Ernle Chatfield,[2] Lieutenant (Sir) Arthur Bromley and others, who afterwards distinguished themselves. These manœuvres enabled the official representatives of the newspapers to look into the heart of the Navy and to write in a manner which would have been otherwise impossible. Those days at sea were a mental as well as a physical tonic. They were full of incident and amusement. They meant little work for me.

One sham battle I have never forgotten. It was a dark night, and the call to "Action Stations" was sounded. The *Good Hope*, in which I was quartered, flew the flag of Admiral Sir Wilmot Fawkes, Charles Madden, newly promoted, being the captain. With great zeal the cruiser opened fire on the enemy. A spirited action was fought. Everyone returned to the wardroom in the early hours of the morning well pleased with the night's work. It was not until later that we learnt that we had fought and sunk —on paper—one of our own side owing to some mistake in the recognition signal! Madden asked me what I should write about the battle. I told him that the Admiralty would no doubt see that appropriate steps were taken

[1] Afterwards Admiral of the Fleet Sir Charles Madden, Bt., G.C.B.

[2] When First Sea Lord, Admiral of the Fleet Sir Ernle (afterwards Lord) Chatfield presided at the Royal United Service Institution when I gave a lecture on merchant shipping.

to prevent the recurrence of such a mistake, and that so far as I was concerned the night had been without incident.

My action, or rather lack of action, meant that I lost the *Daily Telegraph* an article which would have caused some amusement and perhaps dismay. But I never regretted my sacrifice of a good story, nor, I think, did the captain of the *Good Hope*—whom I was to know in later years as the brother-in-law and Chief of Staff of the Commander-in-Chief of the Grand Fleet, Lord Jellicoe—ever forget it. It was characteristic of Madden that on Jellicoe's going to the Admiralty as First Sea Lord in 1916, he remained behind, at the request of Beatty, as second in command. After the signing of the Peace Treaty, he succeeded to the command. It was his difficult task to shake the Fleet down to peace conditions—how difficult it was is known only to the officers who were serving at sea at the time and to the Sea Lords of the Admiralty.

For many years I was reminded of my Plymouth associations by meeting Lord Merivale and Sir Edward Clarke. The former, as Henry Duke, had begun his career as a reporter on the *Western Morning News*. It was then the custom for that paper to have a representative in the gallery of the House of Commons to report the speeches of the M.P.s representing constituencies in Devon and Cornwall. My father-in-law, Albert Groser, sent Duke to London for this work, and thus he met Sir Edward Clarke, one of the members for Plymouth. The latter took a fancy to the young reporter, and suggested that, if he read for the Bar in his spare time, he might be of help to him in his legal career. Thus it happened that Duke became a barrister, entered the House of Commons, was appointed Solicitor-General, served as Irish Secretary and was at length made President of the Admiralty, Probate and Divorce division, in which in due course my son-in-law, Gordon Willmer, K.C., afterwards practised. As an authority on maritime law, the former reporter gained a high reputation. He presided over several international conferences and rendered the world of shipping notable service. When he was raised to the peerage, he chose as his title the little Dartmoor village of Merivale where he had been born. In his later days I met him frequently walking to and from the Law Courts.

I realised his romantic career when I occasionally met Sir Edward Clarke at dinners of the Worshipful Company of Shipwrights, of which I had been made an honorary freeman. It was always a pleasant evening for me when I sat next to the former M.P. for Plymouth and talked of old days. I was present when Sir Edward Clarke made what, I believe, was his last speech. An old man, he retained the silvery tones which had become so familiar in the Law Courts and on the platform, and spoke with that even flow of eloquence which had charmed the electors in Devonshire in former years. But for the sympathy he expressed for the Boers during the South African War, he would probably have held higher office than that of Solicitor-General. That deviation from party allegiance robbed him of any chance of further office. But he was a man whom to know was to respect.

It is a source of some pride to me that I had a small part in the foundation of King George's Fund for Sailors. I had written almost daily in the *Daily Telegraph* on the progress of the war by sea from its opening to the Armistice in 1918. After the German Fleet had been defeated in the Battle of Jutland, the brunt of the struggle fell on merchant seamen and the crews of the Auxiliary Patrol, and it was to their heroic services that I devoted most attention. There was no parallel in history to the manner in which 14,000 seamen laid down their lives, murdered by the enemy's U-boats, which operated without regard to the laws of God or man. After this country had been saved from starvation by the courage and self-sacrifice of these men, Captain George Clark, an Elder Brother of Trinity House, who had served in command of many merchant ships, was seized with the idea that the country should commemorate them by something better than a structure in marble or stone, which would do no good to anyone. He drew up a scheme for setting up an organisation which would do for seamen's charities much the same work as was done by King Edward's Hospital Fund for London for the hospitals.

One day Captain George Clark called on Lord Burnham to ask if the *Daily Telegraph* would advocate the scheme. He had worked out the broad details, and my "chief" was impressed by all that he said and promised his support. I received instructions to prepare an article explaining the proposal from material which Clark supplied, and to write a leader pleading the cause of the seamen. It was the first of several articles on the subject. I was thus brought into close touch with Clark, who was a typical British seaman with a first-class head on his shoulders. He was a tireless worker in the cause, who insisted on things being done "at the double." His favourite exclamation when anyone was causing trouble over some small matter would be, "Now don't make a song and dance about it; let us get on with the job." We consorted together for several months while he was completing his plans, and then, my task done, I disappeared.

Clark, with more influential helpers, went forward in a conquering spirit. His persistency and resourcefulness at length prevailed. Stage by stage his scheme developed. He gained the support of leaders in the shipping world, as well as of others; and at last King George's Fund for Sailors was launched. Clark, who was afterwards knighted, lived sufficiently long to see his dream, which had seemed hopelessly grandiose to some people, realised in an organisation which has since brought vast sums of money to the coffers of the seamen's charities throughout the country. That fund is a far more fitting tribute to the seamen of our race than the official memorial which stands on Tower Hill, where few people but seamen of a later generation see it from year's end to year's end.

During my later years on the *Daily Telegraph* I always

consulted Lord Burnham before undertaking any work other than for that paper. Towards the end of the Great War, as we in our innocence called it, I was invited, with the backing of the Admiralty and the Board of Trade, to write the official history of the part which the Merchant Navy had taken in the struggle. The naval history was well under way, Sir Julian Corbett having been chosen for the task; the record of the movement of seaborne commerce had been entrusted to Mr. C. Ernest Fayle; and a military history was in course of preparation. Should I accept the invitation? I asked Lord Burnham if he had any objection so long as the work did not interfere with my duties on his paper. With characteristic broadmindedness and generosity, he wished me God-speed in the task.

I did not realise when I undertook the preparation of the history that I was nearly at the end of my association with the *Daily Telegraph*. But in 1927 I had a serious illness, which led the doctor to decide that the long and late hours of daily journalism were too much of a strain for me. Consequently, at the end of that year I resigned, and nine days later it was announced that the paper had been sold to Sir William Berry—now Lord Camrose. A new and, as events have proved, a brilliant chapter opened in the history of the journal. Almost from the very day that I left the office, the paper took a new lease of life. Anyone can form his own conclusion as to the connection between the two events. It was no doubt the courageous decision to revert to the old price of one penny which led to the rise of the circulation by leaps and bounds to a figure never before attained by a serious daily journal, with a good prospect of reaching the million mark when the war broke out in 1939, bringing with it a restriction in the supply of newsprint—much coming from Scandinavia—and the unique development of a newspaper purposely cutting down its circulation instead of seeking to increase it.

Probably the *Daily Telegraph* would also have found a place in the same cemetery as so many other newspapers had not Lord Burnham—who, in a fine spirit of patriotism, had accepted an invitation to join the Simon Commission on the future government of India—sold it to Lord Camrose on the eve of sailing. Apart from other services which he has rendered the nation, Lord Camrose gave new life to a newspaper that had claimed to have "the largest circulation in the world." The boast had once, no doubt, been well founded. With the same managing editor as in the last days of the Burnham régime—Arthur E. Watson—the *Daily Telegraph,* with new offices, new printing machinery and a brighter presentation of the news of the day, but much the same attitude towards public affairs, rapidly increased its circle of readers. It is to-day, as it was at the time when I first became associated with it, "a national institution."

When a peerage was conferred on Lord Camrose, whom I knew only slightly, I suggested to him that I hoped he might receive a step in rank for giving London a new evening paper. When I moved from Plymouth to London there were ten of them, all flourishing. Now there are only three, a very limited choice for a population of about 8,000,000 people. His reply was short and conclusive. Before such a venture could be considered, about a million pounds would have to be provided—and risked. So London will have to wait a long time for another evening paper.

CHAPTER III

THE ADMIRAL OF THE FLEET

WHILE I was at Plymouth I saw the Royal Navy at work day by day, but on removing to London I began to study it from another angle—that of the Admiralty. It was a somewhat embarrassing experience, for in those days the naval officer engaged on his duties at sea or in port grumbled a good deal about the ways of the naval authorities in London. I was to learn that there are two sides to every controversy, and that those who give orders are sometimes wiser than those who have to carry them out, believing them to be mistaken.

At the beginning of the century the Admiralty was— Fisher. There were hundreds of other people in the building at Whitehall, naval officers and civil servants, as well, of course, as the First Lord, the Civil Lord and the Financial Secretary, the last three politicians. But John Arbuthnot Fisher was "the Admiral of the Fleet," the man whose word was the law of the Navy. He was the dictator who brooked no disobedience by subordinates, and won by persuasive words the agreement of his colleagues and political masters, from the Prime Minister down to the humblest M.P. who showed signs of opposition to his revolutionary ideas.

Future generations will know little of what they owe to John Arbuthnot, Lord Fisher of Kilverstone. Among the collection of eye-arresting monuments in Westminster Abbey, there is none to perpetuate his memory; St. Paul's Cathedral, where Nelson was laid to rest, has as yet nothing to remind the visitor of all that Fisher did for the nation. I doubt if ever there was a man like him—sailor, administrator, writer and speaker. He was a man of many friends, who would have done anything for him, and of many enemies, who never wearied of reviling him and his works. And yet he triumphed over all calumny and criticism.

On the foundations of the Old Navy, which had won the Battle of Trafalgar and had since rested on its laurels, he created the New Navy, which in the years 1914–18 confronted the fleet of Germany, comparable with it in strength and trained in all the methods of modern warfare. For a period of a quarter of a century, he was the leader of a movement of naval reform which embraced everything ashore and afloat—the administration at Whitehall, the organisation of the Royal Dockyards, the training of officers and men, the design and construction of men-of-war, the composition and distribution of the fleets and squadrons, and the tactics to be employed in action. If it had not been for Fisher's reforming zeal, it is as certain as the setting of the sun each evening that this country would have been defeated by Germany. For every effort in the struggle which opened on August 4th, 1914, rested, in the last analysis, on the sufficiency and efficiency of the Royal Navy.

Though on his father's side he came of an old family which had produced one baronet, Fisher owed nothing to influence or wealth, but everything to his Creator and his own unconquerable spirit. As he said, "I entered the Navy penniless, friendless and forlorn. I have had to fight like hell, and fighting like hell has made me what I am." It seemed as though the spirits of several men of differing character had made their homes in his one body. Sometimes he would be as stern as a judge pronouncing sentence of death; at other times he would look like the typical sand-boy, thoroughly enjoying himself, his face one broad, genial smile; or again, he could be as persuasive as a young man pleading for his lady's love. He was never the same man for two days together, but all that he did he did always whole-heartedly. Even when he sat talking to me in his study in Queen Anne's Gate of an evening, smoking a cigarette and apparently idle, his mind was working. It was never at rest. The story is told that he had two tablets by his bedside—one with a red pencil, which meant "urgent," and the other with a black pencil—and that in the night he would wake and make a note on one or other of the tablets or ask his wife to do so. Fortunately, Lady Fisher was a queen among women, with a dignity that I have never known to be excelled in anyone, imperturbability of temper and, above all, a kind and understanding heart.

Born in far-away Ceylon, Fisher was trained in the Old Navy, where the officers, if not the seamen, had a comfortable, easy-going life. He entered it as a boy of thirteen years, when a youngster to-day would be passing from his preparatory to his public school, shaking perhaps with fear at the prospect. He was tossed on the sea of life in the casual way of those days. He was sent to England without any escort to look after him. "All the entrance examination I had to pass was to write out the Lord's Prayer, do a rule-of-three sum and drink a glass of sherry." The last of Nelson's captains, Admiral Sir William Parker, gave him a nomination for the Navy, and he joined Nelson's flagship, the *Victory*, the most famous ship since the Ark of Noah's day, on June 12th, 1854. It was in that ship that his flag was flown for the last time in 1904, a privilege that custom permitted, when he became First Sea Lord of the Admiralty.

In the intervening years he had taken part in the Crimean and China Wars and the bombardment of Alexandria, mastered the modern gun and introduced the torpedo into the service (founding the present torpedo training ship). He had also served as Director of Naval Ordnance at the Admiralty, as Controller of the Navy and had commanded the North American Squadron and the Mediterranean Fleet successively. All this time he was studying every detail of naval administration and command. While Commander-in-Chief in the Mediterranean from 1899 to 1902, he gathered round him younger officers of brains, and passed under review a long list of reforms, the adoption of which necessarily involved a revolution. He realised that such changes as he contemplated could come only after a long and stern fight, but he was not dismayed by the prospect—indeed, he looked forward with gusto to the struggle against the conservative forces in the naval service as well as in the country.

When the statesmen of the Allied Powers were assembled at Versailles in 1919, a civil servant remarked to me that, though the British people might not realise it until the story of the Old Navy and the New Navy came to be written in perspective and without personal bias, the war of 1914–18 had, in fact, been won before a gun had been fired in anger—won by Fisher and the officers who had been associated with him. "He was the man," he added, "who foresaw that war was coming, reformed the naval adminis-tration, introduced the 'Dreadnought' design of battleship with increased draught and beam, which delayed the war's opening until he had got the Royal Navy ready for the ordeal, and, years in advance, picked a young and compara-tively unknown officer, John Rushworth Jellicoe, as Com-mander-in-Chief of the Grand Fleet." The foundations of victory at sea, and it was victory at sea that determined the issue of the war, were laid in the preceding years of peace by an invincible quartet—John Arbuthnot Fisher, John Rushworth Jellicoe, Reginald Bacon and Percy Scott, and in the background was a former officer of the Royal Marines, Maurice Hankey,[1] who by the influence of Fisher in the day of his greatest power had been appointed Secretary of the Committee of Imperial Defence.

I was still at Plymouth in the closing years of the nine-teenth century when I first became acquainted with Fisher, who was then Commander-in-Chief at Portsmouth. Some incident had led me to wonder whether in composi-tion, manning and distribution the Fleet was such as to give an assurance of victory if we became involved in war. Knowing little of strategy or tactics, I put my crude

[1] Raised to the peerage as Lord Hankey in 1939.

ideas on paper and sent them to him. I was gratified by receiving an acknowledgment of my scheme, was bluntly told that Fisher had a better one, and that some day he would tell me about it. A link was thus formed which was not broken until I attended the memorial service in Westminster Abbey, when the "Last Post" rang out.

This is not the occasion for writing a biography of Fisher. That task has been done, and well done.[2] No words can adequately describe him as he was known to his friends in his various moods. He was a man of the world, who could deal with politicians with their own weapons and defeat them. In pursuit of his ends, he was ruthless and relentless in his relations with subordinates in the Navy, sometimes adopting means which squeamish friends thought unjustified. If ever he knew a doubt or fear in his life, he never showed evidence of it. When he was satisfied that something had to be done, he did it regardless of consequences to himself or his career. He might have retired from the Navy and made a fortune in the business world, for he had many offers, but his high sense of patriotism restrained him. Many honours came to him, and they pleased and amused him. When he wore so many decorations on State occasions that he looked, as he said himself, like a Christmas tree, his pride was not in his personal success, but in the services which he had rendered to his country. Looking back, I believe that he owed much of his steadfastness of purpose and resilience of spirit in days of controversy to the many half-hours he spent in the peace and quiet of Westminster Abbey or St. Paul's Cathedral. He was "a sermon taster," and would go to hear any preacher, whatever his denomination, who had a message to give.

My friendship with him lasted for over twenty unclouded years, with one short passage at arms when, in his old age, he denounced me on the telephone as "a traitor to your country." That was because I declined to support an

[2] "Lord Fisher, Admiral of the Fleet." A biography by Admiral Sir R. H. Bacon.

agitation for his return to the Admiralty towards the end of the war of 1914–18. Some politicians, in pursuit of their own ends, had suggested that he should become, not First Sea Lord, but First Lord—the political head of the Admiralty—hoping to profit by his reputation as an administrator who got things done. He had already filled the position of First Sea Lord for two terms, and had regretted his hasty resignation on the last occasion. He was impatient to be once more in control of naval affairs, and it was, therefore, perhaps natural that he should turn a willing ear to such suggestions. But one of his oldest friends, knowing of the intrigue, warned me that, as I valued his reputation and had regard to the interests of the country, I should lend no hand in furthering this design. The breach was, happily, only temporary.

He seldom spoke in public. He may be said, indeed, to have made only one speech in his life, apart from two short statements in the House of Lords late in his official career, when he explained why he would not try to excuse his action in particular matters. The occasion of his one speech was the Royal Academy Banquet in 1903. Fisher was then in the thick of fierce controversy over his naval reforms; his enemies had not yet mobilised their forces against him, and he was something of a hero in the eyes of his fellow countrymen, who were beginning to get nervous owing to the steady expansion of the German Fleet. That speech revealed Fisher in a confident, humorous mood, when he thought a joke better conveyed his serious purpose than words of portentous warning.

He told his hearers that when he first went to sea in an old sailing two-decker, he saw inscribed in great big gold letters the one word "Silence," and underneath was the phrase, "Deeds, not words." He said that he had put that admonition in every ship he had commanded since. "This leads me," he continued, "to another motto which is better still."

When I was Commander-in-Chief in the Mediterranean,

I went to inspect a small destroyer, only 260 tons, but with such pride and swagger that she might have been of 16,000 tons. The young lieutenant in command took me round. She was in beautiful order, and I came aft to the wheel and saw there the inscription: "Ut Veniant Omnes." "Hallo," I said, "what the deuce is that?" Saluting me, he said, "Let 'em all come, sir." Well, that was not boasting; that was the sense of conscious efficiency—the sense that permeates the whole Fleet—and I used to think as an admiral, it will be irresistible provided the admiral is up to the mark.

With these introductory words, which were greeted with cheers, he went on:

But what I wish to remark to you is this—and it is a good thing for everybody to know it—there has been a tremendous change in naval matters since the old time. In regard to naval warfare, history is a record of exploded ideas. In the old days they were sailors' battles; now they are admirals' battles. I should like to recall to you the greatest battle at sea ever fought. What was the central episode of that? Nelson receiving his death wound! What was he doing? Walking up and down on the quarter-deck arm-in-arm with his captain. It is dramatically described to us by an onlooker. His secretary is shot down: Nelson turns round and says, "Poor Scott! Take him down to the cockpit," and then he goes on walking up and down, having a yarn with his captain. What does that mean? It means that in the old days the admiral took his fleet into action: each ship got alongside the enemy; and, as Nelson finely said, "They got into their proper place." And then the admiral had not much more to do. The ships were touching one another nearly, the bos'un went with some rope and lashed them together so as to make them quite comfortable —and the sailors loaded and fired away till it was time to board.

But what is the case now? It is conceivable that within twenty minutes of sighting the enemy on the horizon, the action will have begun, and on the disposition of his Fleet by the admiral—on his tactics—the battle will depend, for all the gunnery in the world is no good if the guns are

5

masked by our own ships or cannot bear on the enemy!
In that way I wish to tell you how much depends on the
admirals now and on their education. Therefore, joined
with this spirit, of which the remark of the young lieutenant
I mentioned to you is an indication, permeating the whole
Service, we require a fearless, vigorous and progressive
administration, open to any reform, never resting on its
oars—for to stop is to go back—and forecasting every
eventuality.

Then he discussed the coming of the submarine and
wireless telegraphy: "In their inception they were the
weapons of the weak, now they loom large as the weapons
of the strong."

Is there the slightest fear of invasion with them, even
for the most extreme pessimist? I might mention other
subjects; but the great fact which I come to is that we are
realising—the Navy and the Admiralty are realising—*that
on the British Navy rests the British Empire*. Nothing else
is of any use without it, not even the Army. We are
different from continental nations. No soldier of ours can
go anywhere unless a sailor carries him there on his back.
I am not disparaging the Army. I am looking forward to
their coming to sea with us again, as they did in the old
days. Why, Nelson had three regiments of infantry with
him at the Battle of Cape St. Vincent, and a sergeant of the
69th Regiment led the boarders, and Nelson having only
one arm, it was the sergeant who helped him up. The
Secretary for War particularly asked me to allude to the
Army, or else I would not have done it!
In conclusion, I assure you that the Navy and the
Admiralty recognise their responsibility. I think I may say
that we now have a Board of Admiralty that is united, progressive and determined—and you may sleep quietly in
your beds.

His final words, though received with cheers when they
were spoken, afterwards raised a storm of protest from "the
old ladies of both sexes," as he described them. They held
up their hands in horror at his assurance that they could

rest quietly in their beds. Was that the way to steel the nation to war, if war was to come? Fisher, sure of the work of reform on which he was engaged, was not perturbed. He had no doubts. He realised what modern naval warfare would mean, with the battle gun fired at a range of fifteen miles or so and the automobile torpedo travelling swiftly to its target beneath the surface of the sea. He was satisfied that when the day came the instrument of sea power which he was forging would, in the hands of Jellicoe, as Commander-in-Chief, not fail to seize and maintain the command of the sea against all comers.

A phrase of Fisher's, of which a great deal of play was made at this period, when he had gathered round him a group of officers on whose ability he felt he could rely, was "Favouritism is the secret of efficiency." It was said that this exposed the weakness of his administration at the Admiralty; he was surrounded by his favourites—what the Americans call "yes men." But Fisher's statement was a reasonable one. Anyone in a position of authority inevitably calls to his aid men he knows well, whom he has tested and in whose loyalty he can place confidence. That is particularly necessary when a series of co-ordinated and complicated schemes are to be carried out, and carried out without loss of time. Fisher believed that Germany might begin war before the British Navy could be made "instantly ready for war." Speed in execution of the work in hand was therefore necessary, and so he gathered round him officers who were in sympathy with his ideas and would work with a will.

Only those whose memories go back to the condition of the Navy in the later years of the nineteenth century can form any conception of the character and extent of the work which was carried out under Fisher's leadership, with the active goodwill of King Edward VII, who never lost faith in the naval officer who had convinced him that, unless revolutionary changes were made, the trident would pass into the hands of his nephew, the Emperor William II. His

Majesty had known the Emperor intimately since, as a boy, he had been a frequent visitor to Queen Victoria, his grandmother, and he had no illusions as to his ambitions. As a guest at Osborne House, the Queen's summer residence, the future Kaiser had wandered about Portsmouth Dockyard, visited men-of-war when under refit, and watched them pass in and out of Spithead. King Edward was suspicious of his nephew's ambitions, and backed up Fisher through thick and thin. When His Majesty passed away in 1910, Fisher wrote to me, "I am utterly capsized by the King's death; no one can ever know what a staunch friend he was to me." [1] The public did not realise it, for the *Court Circular* was silent on the matter, but Fisher was a frequent visitor at Buckingham Palace to the King, whom he loved and for whose political wisdom and long-sightedness he had unbounded admiration.

Before Fisher began to wield his reforming broom, the Royal Navy was living in the past. It was "the spit and polish" era. What mattered was that the ships should look smart. Gunnery was regarded as of slight importance; the torpedo was a nuisance. It was said that one admiral always wore white gloves during his periodical inspections of the ships under his command. When he had been all over a ship, he would hold out his gloved hands to the captain and exclaim, "There, sir, is your report." That officer knew by the marks of dirt whether he would have a good or a bad report. As an illustration, the report of an admiral after inspecting a ship in the autumn of 1901 may be mentioned. It referred to the physique of the ship's company, their cleanliness—the state of their bedding being noted as "specially satisfactory." It added that "at exercise the men moved very smartly"; that the ship looked well inside and

[1] In the same letter, he declared, "Remember, 'Repetition is the soul of Journalism'; keep on reiterating what you *have* said while putting in new stuff! . . . Also rub in again and again, ' *Starvation, not Invasion.*' That's a battle cry! 'Sea Predominance is the *one* and *only* aim.' '*The one thing needful,*' and then follows 'Perspective.' The d—d rot of a big Army! What for?"

out, and that the admiral found the tone of the ship to be "distinctly good." No reference was made to the fighting equipment of this man-of-war, or to the smart manner in which gunnery practice had been carried out.

That was typical of the period. "It was only success in tailoring and house-maiding and the state of the bedding," Scott claimed, "that gained commendation." Arnold White, a journalist who wrote fearlessly in the *Referee* and in other papers, once declared that because gunnery practice was apt to make a mess, ammunition was sometimes thrown overboard. His statement was challenged, and before an impartial referee he proved his words by irrefutable evidence. Such was the indifference of many senior officers that commanders knew that paint was the important consideration if they were to secure promotion, and the seamen were kept so continually at work plastering their ship with paint that after several years in service her draught would be increased appreciably.

In those days much of the cost of the paint needed to keep a ship smart fell on the commander, who knew that promotion depended on the way in which his ship struck the eye of his admiral. The official allowance was small. One young officer of slender means—Charles —— was indebted to his aunt, who had faith in his future, for the necessary money to enable him to buy sufficient paint. This lady, who was known as "Charley's Aunt" in the Service, would turn up from time to time, ostensibly to visit her nephew, but really, it was concluded, to see that her money was being spent on paint.

The Navy was living on its old tradition, handed down from the Napoleonic Wars. The principal squadrons, consisting of the newest and most powerful ships, were stationed in the Mediterranean; in the other seas there was a curious assortment of ships which were known as "bug traps," which could neither fight nor run away. The administration of the dockyards was archaic. Expenditure on the naval administration was high, because so many ships, officers and

men were wasted. The conduct of the Royal Navy's affairs
was inefficient. There were no war plans, and no one in
authority was disturbed. The Admiralty was a place of
circumlocutory ways—anything to delay progress. It was a
comfortable régime, and only a few far-seeing officers realised
that it had to be changed. Fisher swept away the cobwebs
as well as the spiders.

Several years before Fisher came into power at the
Admiralty, an unknown naval officer, Percy Scott, had
turned his attention to gunnery. Most officers knew little
or nothing about it. He made it a matter of close study
after the Fleet had made a very poor exhibition at the
bombardment of Alexandria. The conclusions he came to
were that the gun-sights were out of date, that the gun-
mountings left much to be desired, that the range at which
practice took place was too short—and, in brief, that there
was a great deal of leeway to be made up. He was of an
inventive mind, and he designed a number of devices which
he believed would increase the rate and accuracy of fire at
longer ranges. Towards the end of the nineteenth century, when Percy Scott was in command of the cruiser
Scylla in the Mediterranean, he showed what could be done
if his system of training were adopted.

At that time the usual signal of an admiral to his fleet
was, "Spread for target practice; expend a quarter's ammunition, and rejoin my flag (at such and such a place and
time)." When Scott's ship took part in the usual target
practice, it scored so heavily—eighty per cent. of hits—that
it was suggested by some ill-natured persons that there must
have been some hanky-panky. Subsequently, on the China
station, he repeated his triumph when captain of the cruiser
Terrible.

Gradually the Admiralty began to take an interest in
gunnery, especially as Scott's methods had been approved
by such officers as Prince Louis of Battenberg, Jellicoe,
then only a captain, and other coming men. When he
returned home, Scott began an agitation for gunnery

reform, using the newspapers in order to shame the authorities into action. It was at this stage of the movement that I came across Scott. He was a man of note, full of enthusiasm for one thing only—improving the gunnery of the Fleet. He was not *persona grata* with most of his contemporaries in the Service, but he cared little for that. He worked on unconcerned, his friends on the newspapers using the ammunition with which he supplied them.

His reward came early in 1905, when a new office was created at the Admiralty—that of Inspector of Target Practice—in order that Scott might, by going from fleet to fleet, show the Navy how to shoot. He was directly under the First Sea Lord, then Fisher, and not under the Board of Admiralty. When the announcement was made, Mr. Gibson Bowles, an outspoken M.P., remarked that this officer "had made the gunnery of the Navy in spite of the Admiralty," and enquired what his duties were, "since he was rather a wild animal to let loose on a tame Board of Admiralty." But the Admiralty was no longer "tame." Fisher was in control. As Fisher had created the new office, not the least important of his reforms, Scott was left in no doubt as to what he should do. He drew up new rules, and personally attended all the firings of the three principal Fleets. He had the results published, and the newspapers made the most of the information. A spirit of emulation in the Navy was aroused. The gunnery of the Fleet steadily improved in subsequent years, and as a result of Scott's agitation and the support of Fisher and Jellicoe, gunnery took its rightful place in the training of the New Navy for war.

How fierce the struggle had been in which Scott engaged I did not realise until I edited his autobiography. In looking through the papers he placed at my disposal, I came to know how bitterly he had been maligned by those whom he regarded as "the Old School." His creed was a simple one, which every naval officer to-day accepts. A man-of-war is designed, built and manned in order to fight, and everything else must be subordinated to that purpose; in so far as "spit and polish" can contribute to that end, they are desirable.

This movement for gunnery efficiency, as I have remarked, was under way while Fisher was working out his great schemes of reform, which included ships that could fight more effectively at long ranges than the vessels then at sea. In a word, Fisher planned to take the whole Navy, shake it out of its ill-founded complacency, change the spirit of the Admiralty, alter the system of training officers of all ranks, and place in an efficient state the Royal Dockyards. They still kept boarding pikes in stock because they had been used in Nelson's day, and had machinery for building men-of-war and repairing them which was hopelessly out of date.

I moved to London at a moment when the outcry occasioned by the naval reforms which were then being carried out was gathering force and cohesion, restrained only by the knowledge that Fisher had gained support in the highest quarters, political as well as social. I shall always look back with pride on the freedom which Lord Burnham—the first Lord Burnham—and Le Sage gave me to fight for the Fisher policy in the *Daily Telegraph* and elsewhere, though they were, no doubt, aware of the taunt that I was in "the Fish Pond." The consequences of defeat at sea by the rapidly increasing German Fleet filled me with anxiety, and by every means I endeavoured to carry on the work which had been begun by W. H. Stead, Arnold White and others.

My zeal, possibly intemperate, led me to use every avenue that was open to me to influence public opinion. At last I raised, quite unconsciously, a storm of which the echoes were heard in the House of Commons. I wrote and published anonymously a brochure under the title "The Truth About the Navy." It was widely circulated; then Fisher took a hand in gaining a larger public for a publication which revealed what the Old Navy had been like and what the

New Navy would be like when the work of reform had been completed. There were questions in Parliament, and a great deal of dust was stirred up in the hope that Fisher would be frightened—as though anyone had ever frightened him from taking the course on which he had set out.

I recall a story which illustrates his methods. It may be apochryphal, but it may well be true. He brought back to the Admiralty when he gave up the command of the Mediterranean the design of the all-big-gun ship which afterwards became known as the "Dreadnought" class. He sensed the clamour which would be raised at the abandonment of the ideas on mixed armament which had hitherto guided the Admiralty. So he decided to remit his plan to a strong committee of naval officers (including Jellicoe), scientists, shipbuilders and others. It is said that on the morning when the first meeting was to be held, he sent for Jellicoe to talk matters over, and handed to him a document as they parted, saying, "Here is the report." As a matter of fact, the enquiry was of a most searching character, many experiments were made and some modifications were introduced. But, in essence, the *Dreadnought* which dismayed the Germans and upset all their calculations was in most respects the type of ship which Fisher's fertile brain had conceived.

A story hangs by the revolution in design embodied in the "Dreadnought" battle-cruiser, a type of ship with the heavy armament of a battleship and the high speed of a cruiser. The tale goes that Fisher suspected that the Germans would try to discover the secrets of its construction and armament. So he had alternative plans prepared, and arranged that they should be left about in Portsmouth Dockyard, where an enemy agent might easily get hold of them. In the event, these plans were stolen, the German Admiralty accepted them as authentic, a ship was built which it was believed would resemble the earliest of the "Dreadnought" battle-cruisers, and, owing to its weakness, that man-of-war, the *Blucher*, was sunk at Jutland. I have been told that this incident has no foundation, but it might well be true, because it is characteristic of Fisher's methods. Fisher delighted in outmanœuvring the Germans, and particularly Von Tirpitz, and of all Englishmen he was the one who gave them most cause for worry.

The question has often been asked: "Why were the 'Dreadnoughts' built?" The answer is that such ships— all-big-gun ships—could deliver a greater weight of metal in a given time, at a longer range, than could the men-of-war with a mixed armament of 12-in., 9.2-in. and 6-in. guns which had been favoured hitherto throughout the world. Once the building of the original *Dreadnought* had begun, the Germans had to possess ships of the same type in the spirit of rivalry which was then current. But they wanted to be able to move the fleet rapidly between the Baltic and the North Sea. That facility was the basis of their strategy. As the *Dreadnought* was of greater displacement, length and beam than any ships then in the German Fleet, that meant widening the Kiel Canal, for it was too shallow and too narrow for the new type, and that was a matter of time —a long time.

The original *Dreadnought*, which was completed in a year and a day from the laying of the keel plates, made history. King Edward VII, it seemed to me, realised the significance of the occasion when, in the uniform of Admiral of the Fleet, he launched her at Portsmouth on February 10th, 1906. It was a memorable day. At an early hour in the morning a fierce hurricane swept over the town, accompanied by heavy driving rain, as though everything was conspiring to spoil the ceremony. All concerned in the event listened to the howling wind and watched the driving rain with feelings of deep depression. As the morning advanced, however, the rain ceased, the clouds dispersed, and the sun shone fitfully on the tens of thousands of ticket holders and the general public as they hurried towards the dockyard. Once again the good fortune usually attending King Edward when he discharged a public duty which necessarily exposed him to the inclemency of the weather was vouchsafed to him. The short proceedings, full as they were of deep significance to the future of the navies of the world, passed off with complete success.

His Majesty afterwards indicated once more the close personal interest which he took in the well-being of the country's first line of defence by honouring the two officers who had been largely responsible for the spirit of enthusiasm for straight, quick shooting which was by then spreading through the fleets and squadrons of the Royal Navy. After the launch, he conferred the Knight Commandership of the Royal Victorian Order upon Rear-Admiral Percy Scott, whose appointment as Inspector of Target Practice had proved to be one of the happiest inspirations of the Board of Admiralty. At the same time, Captain J. Rushworth Jellicoe, C.B., the Director of Naval Ordnance, who had encouraged the movement, received from the hands of His Majesty the Order of Commander of the Victorian Order, in recognition of his devotion and skill.

The launch is fixed in my memory, because when it came to singing the seamen's hymn, "For those in peril on the sea," Fisher shared a hymn-sheet with His Majesty. I could not believe that another was not available. It struck me that the First Sea Lord had possibly taken care that it should not be offered to King Edward, so that they might sing together. Fisher was supreme as a stage manager. The reviews at Spithead which were held during his service at the Admiralty were triumphs of organisation, and for that reason all the more impressive.

The building of the New Navy, which was to hold the seas against the Germans in 1914–18, had begun. The "Dreadnought" did more than render the Kiel Canal useless for the time; it suspended the construction of battleships in every foreign country for nearly two years, until the secret of the new design could be ascertained. It raised the prestige of the Royal Navy, because it reminded the world that Great Britain meant business, and would fight at longer ranges than had been thought possible. This ship—the forerunner of many embodying the same principles, laid down in succeeding years—had 12-in. guns, turbine machinery giving greater speed and she was more heavily armoured than her predecessors. The design was the expression of the First Sea Lord's maxim—"Hit first, hit hard and keep on hitting." Fisher made the most of his "secret"; and foreign naval authorities were led to pause, wondering what was happening in the country that had preserved its ancient naval traditions while Germany and other countries had been forging ahead.

If it cannot be said that the naval world was hood-winked by Fisher's dramatic move, the effect of his intro-duction of the "Dreadnought" came very near to it. For the main idea of the design had been evolved by an Italian naval constructor some time before, and the all-big-gun ship was the obvious deduction from the theories of gunnery which Percy Scott had developed. But, in any case, the Admiralties of the world were thrown into con-fusion, with the result that while we went on with the task of building the New Navy—battleships and battle-cruisers embodying the "Dreadnought" ideas—they felt compelled to stop work in the shipyards for fear of sur-prises to be sprung upon them by the naval officer in Whitehall, the mystery man whose ways they could not understand.

CHAPTER IV

THE MARCH OF NAVAL REFORM

THE rebuilding of the Royal Navy was the sequel to the series of administrative reforms which Fisher had instituted. As First Lord of the Admiralty, the Earl of Selborne has never received the acknowledgment due to him for the courageous step he took in deciding that the old order had to give place to the new. Possibly that is because he was not an effective platform speaker, and did not claim any credit for his work. He was not dramatic in his methods, believing in evolution rather than revolution. He had served with Joseph Chamberlain at the Colonial Office, and had been seized with a true conception of the dependence of the Empire on sea power. He had, moreover, become convinced that a reform of the tariff of this country, with some form of Imperial Preference, was essential in the interest alike of our industries, then being increasingly menaced by foreign protective measures, and of the Dominions and Colonies seeking markets for their goods.

Lord Selborne was appointed First Lord of the Admiralty in 1900, the year in which the second of the series of German Navy Acts was passed. He remained in office for five years. His conversion to the necessity of a change in naval policy began in 1901 when he visited Malta, the base of the Mediterranean Fleet which Fisher then commanded, in company with the First Sea Lord (Lord Walter Kerr) and the Director of Naval Intelligence (Rear-Admiral Reginald Custance). The voyage was ostensibly undertaken for the purpose of inspecting the provision to be made for protecting the harbour from torpedo attack, but Fisher had already been in forceful correspondence with the Admiralty on many matters.

Early in the following year, although this Commander-in-Chief had shown that he was an ardent reformer, Lord Selborne invited Fisher to join the Board of Admiralty as Second Sea Lord. This meant that he would have the power to act, and not merely to talk and write. The First Lord thus nailed his colours to the mast as a reformer. A tale is told of Lord Walter Kerr which suggests the unceasing energy of Fisher, who wanted everyone "to go at the double," in the manner of bluejackets when exercising on board ship. After the energetic vice-admiral, as Fisher then was, had been harrying the department for several months with a stream of ideas, all of which he urged should be carried into effect at once, Lord Walter Kerr came into his room, and, placing his hand on his shoulder, said to his old friend, "Jack, don't you think we might have a rest now? I am so tired!"

The new Second Sea Lord immediately developed and began to carry into effect his scheme for the training of officers for the Navy, which resulted in the setting up of a college at Osborne for cadets on entry, who were to go on to the establishment at Dartmouth. Nor was that all. The First Lord agreed that Fisher should become Commander-in-Chief at Portsmouth, in order that he might superintend at close quarters all the proposed changes. Within a year, in spite of all the opposition of the die-hards in the Navy, Fisher returned to the Admiralty as First Sea Lord at the invitation of Lord Selborne. No Minister who wanted peace would have asked him to join the Board.

In the Memorandum in which he explained the Navy Estimates for 1902–3, Lord Selborne defended the calling home from the outer seas of the ships which could neither fight nor run away, and the distribution of the officers and men in the great Fleet which it had been decided that it was necessary to provide in the North Sea and English Channel, in view of the increasing threat of the German Navy. Fisher had not overlooked the statement in the preamble to the Navy Act of 1900 that "it is not absolutely necessary that the German Battle Fleet should be as strong as that of the greatest naval power, for a great naval power will not, as a rule, be in a position to concentrate all its striking force against us."

It is small wonder that Fisher respected the courage and persistence of a statesman who, once having satisfied himself that changes were necessary, held on his course unswervingly. Selborne had no closed mind, but was always open to conviction. Fisher had to win his approval by argument stage by stage. It is said that when on one occasion the First Lord raised objections to a detail in the reform policy, remarking that it was opposed to all precedent, Fisher responded in a flash of wit, "I agree. If Noah were navigating the Ark to-day, do you imagine that he would bring it to rest on the top of Mount Ararat? Certainly not, he would anchor off Monte Carlo."

Fisher often frightened conventional people by his unconventional language, which suggested rashness to the point of folly. The nervous pacifist was shocked when he declared that "War is violence, and moderation in war is imbecility." But violence *is* the very essence of war.

His policy was that the Royal Navy should fight, and not merely look pretty. In these circumstances, when Lord Selborne, by lifting his finger, could have halted the movement, it went forward, finding its most forceful expression in the creation of the Home Fleet. This meant in its final development a change of the naval front from southern to northern waters. Eventually the Home Fleet became the Grand Fleet, which held the keys of sea command throughout the war of 1914–18.

Vital changes were also made in the administrative machinery at the Admiralty. The First Sea Lord's prestige and authority was increased, and every member of the Board was given specific duties. This is not the occasion for painting a complete picture of the naval reforms which were carried out in these years. If it be asked what, in sum total, they amounted to, the words of Lord Balfour in a speech at Glasgow in January 1905 may be quoted: "The fighting power of the British Fleet during the first twenty-four hours, let us say, of hostilities with a foreign power has been augmented not once, or twice, but threefold." It is true that Balfour was in some measure patting himself on the back, for he had supported the reform programme, but later events confirmed his verdict.

I came across Lord Selborne later when he contributed the introduction to a short history of the Royal Navy that I had written at the request of the Central Conservative Office. The party was anxious to provide speakers with a convenient synopsis of the part which our naval power had played in preserving this country from war in years when the Continent had been drenched in blood, and also the influence it had had in the building up and preservation of the Empire. I thought that Lord Selborne would take the matter lightly, but, on the contrary, he was most serious. He was heart and soul "a big Navy man." I remember one doctrine of his in particular. He mentioned it after reading something I had written. "Imperial policy depends upon the strength of the Navy, not, as the Little Englanders so grotesquely imagine, *the size of the Navy on Imperial policy.*"

In a letter in August 1913 he wrote to me:

I do not think there will be any difficulty in the Unionist Party adhering to the Two Keels to One Standard. I quite deliberately did not refer to it in my speech, because I wanted to pin the Government down to their own standard, and because I knew that if I did they would ride off on the general question of expense, as Churchill did in his last speech in the House of Commons.

It will not have escaped your observation that at the present moment, in looking forward to 1915 and 1916, the Two Keels to One Standard means fifty-two ships, and even if you include the *Lord Nelson* and the *Agamemnon* we shall be nine short of that, or eight short if you include the *Australia,* or, if you include the three Canadians, which

San Remo, Belgrave Road,
Torquay. Christmas Day 1923

My dear Hurd,

Many thanks for your letter.
All my best congratulations and
Good Wishes for "The Day"! and Continued
success for the Coming Year —

Your clear duty is to Save the
British Navy from the Spoilers — of any
political party.

Ultimately — Asquith won't win fame by
voting with the Reds to defeat the Gov't —
He ought — in my opinion — to support the Gov't —
and then later on form — perhaps — some sort of
National party to keep out our common foe.

In the Hotel — it really isn't one —
there is an old Portuguese — called Jogo! —
But he is not an Admiral I believe he comes
from Manchester. His owner is a Portuguese ! —

Ever — John M. Le Sage

Myself —
Not at all well — {
No appetite {

Archibald Hurd, Eq'r

FACSIMILE LETTER FROM SIR JOHN M. LE SAGE

H.M.S. "VICTORY" SALUTING THE FIRST "DREADNOUGHT"

Sketch by SIGNOR MARTINO, Marine Painter to Queen Victoria and King Edward VII

are still quite uncertain, we shall be five short. But the
Dominion ships ought to be extra, all of them.

Now that we can look back on the movement which gave
the country the reformed Royal Navy, which was the
foundation of the Allied victory in 1918, tribute should be
paid to Lord Selborne for the work which he did at the
Admiralty. Even when he was no longer in office, he
continued to take a useful part in naval affairs, always
urging the maintenance of a strong Fleet as the basis of
British diplomacy, and as an assurance of the supply of
our food and raw materials and the defence of the whole
Empire.

With Fisher still First Sea Lord, the work of reform
went forward under Lord Cawdor until Balfour's Government passed out of office in July 1902. As this is not a
naval history, it is unnecessary to trace the various stages
of the movement. Fisher saw to it that there was no set-
back.

One service which Fisher did, apart from his work as a
naval reformer, was to father the Committee of Imperial
Defence, of which Captain (afterwards Admiral Sir
Charles) Ottley was secretary in the later days of Fisher's
régime at the Admiralty. I had met him when he was
Director of Naval Intelligence at the Admiralty. Anyone
less like a sailor in appearance it would be difficult to
imagine. He was a small man, of slight build and precise
ways. It seemed as though a Channel breeze might blow
him from any quarter-deck. Fisher had marked him down
as likely to be more useful ashore than afloat. When the
position of secretary to the Committee of Imperial Defence
fell vacant, owing to the retirement of Sir George Clarke—
afterwards Lord Sydenham—who was a soldier, the First
Sea Lord claimed that it was the turn of the Navy to
nominate a successor. Thus Ottley passed across Whitehall
to the offices of the Imperial Defence Committee in Whitehall Gardens. I saw a good deal of him in later years, for

6

he was most friendly and accessible, anxious that I should appreciate the course which defence policy was taking.

The work of the committee was then on comparatively modest lines, for it was not regarded with great favour by many officers at the Admiralty and War Office, who feared it might trench on the action of both these departments. The rank and file of the Liberal Party looked at it askance. Ottley, therefore, walked warily. He was a man of consummate tact and patience. By the time he gave up his position, the committee was firmly established. The principle that the Navy was our first line of defence had been embodied once more in the policy of the nation.

Ottley did notable work at 2, Whitehall Gardens, but he was in a position which carried no pension. One day early in 1912 he telephoned to me that he wanted my advice. When I arrived at his office, he told me that he had received an offer to join the Board of Directors of Armstrong, Whitworth & Co. He had consulted Asquith, then Prime Minister, who had told him that he could not give him any extension beyond the normal age limit which he was approaching. So he resigned.

Who was to be Ottley's successor? The War Office made a claim for the nomination. But Fisher, who was never caught napping, outmanœuvred the soldiers by putting forward the name of a member of Ottley's staff who was a Royal Marine—"a soldier and sailor too" in Kipling's phrase. His choice was Major Maurice Hankey, who had acted as assistant secretary to the committee for four years, revealing qualities of mind as well as amazing industry which marked him out for the succession. Hankey was a son of the Empire. Himself born in Australia, his wife had come from South Africa, the daughter of the Surveyor-General of Cape Colony; after leaving Rugby, he had served as a Royal Marine in various parts of the Empire before going to the Naval Intelligence Department at the Admiralty in 1902. He was the ideal successor to Ottley. Fisher triumphed, fortunately for the country, as later events were to show.

I had met Hankey soon after his removal from the Admiralty to Whitehall Gardens. One day when I was talking to Ottley, a young man whose alert, bright eyes at once attracted me came into the room with some papers. Thus began a friendship which suffered no eclipse when I came, nominally at least, in the sphere of his influence on my undertaking the writing of the official history of the Merchant Navy's part in the war of 1914–18. I was then, in fact, a member of the Historical Section of the Committee of Imperial Defence. Though Colonel E. Y. Daniel was in charge of all the histories, Hankey was our "chief." He was overwhelmed with his more immediate and important duties, so, like the skilled administrator that he was, he trusted Daniel to "carry on."

In order that the importance of Hankey's work as secretary to the Committee of Imperial Defence may be understood, I must turn back several years. The creation of the committee was the inspiration of Balfour. It was to be the clearing-house of ideas of the fighting Services, co-ordinating their plans. It was Hankey who, working in the background of the national stage, gave form and reality to Balfour's dream in the years immediately before the outbreak of the war of 1914–18. Under his inspiration, with the support of successive Prime Ministers whose friendship he gained and retained whether in office or opposition, the Committee of Imperial Defence exercised a powerful influence on common matters of defence, without encroaching unduly upon the separate affairs of either the Admiralty or the War Office.

Fisher once wrote to me, "Hankey has a splendid brain; Esher says he beats Napoleon." History will show that Fisher and Esher were right. This young Royal Marine decided that each department in the State should know exactly what it had to do in the event of hostilities. No such preparation had ever been made before; we had muddled through one war after another. But if we had to fight Germany, we should be opposed to a nation

which had considered every possibility and laid its plans
accordingly.

His solution of the problem was the "War Book."
This was a herculean task, which could be done only with
the co-operation of every public office. A sub-committee
for the "Co-ordination of Departmental Action at the
Outbreak of War" was appointed to strengthen the hands
of the secretary of the main committee. In the gradual
evolution from chaos to order, Balfour and Asquith took
the closest interest; the latter, when Prime Minister, informed the House of Commons of the orderly thinking
and planning which the sub-committee had been doing.

This sub-committee, which is composed of the principal
permanent officials of the various departments of State, has,
after many months of continuous labour, compiled a War
Book. We call it a War Book—and it is a book which
definitely assigns to each department—not merely the War
Office and Admiralty, but the Home Office, the Board of
Trade, and every department of the State—its responsibility for action under every head of war policy. The
departments themselves, in pursuance of the instructions
given by the War Book, have drafted all the proclamations,
Orders in Council, letters, telegrams, notices and so forth,
which can be foreseen. Every possible provision has been
made to avoid delay in setting in force the machinery in
the unhappy event of war taking place. It has been
thought necessary to make this committee permanent, in
order that these war arrangements may be constantly kept
up to date.

The goodwill and the aid of all the chief officials in and
about Whitehall had to be enlisted. Many men of less
determination and tact would have quailed in face of the
obstacles. But Hankey was not dismayed. He and his
staff worked quietly for a long time at the compilation of
this volume. When the war did break out, the War Book
had been completed, with the result that though mistakes
were made, we were ready for hostilities as we had never
been before.

It was the kind of work which appealed not at all to the popular imagination, but it saved the situation when war at last broke out. And in subsequent months, the secretary to the Committee of Imperial Defence, of whose existence the general public had little or no knowledge, took a leading part in shaping the defence policy of the Allies. It was only when the struggle was over and the debt which the country owed to him was paid by the House of Commons, that it was realised that behind the scenes a great brain had been at work before and during the struggle, and that victory had been in some measure due to his knowledge, sagacity and industry.

In order that continuity of policy might be ensured, Hankey became in 1916 the first secretary which the Cabinet had ever had, as hitherto its proceedings had had no recorder. Later he was appointed Clerk of the Privy Council. As secretary to the War Cabinet, when it was founded during the war, and also to successive Imperial Conferences as well as to the Peace Conference, he became the reservoir of more secrets affecting national and Imperial affairs than any man in the public service had possessed. And yet, in conversation, no one would imagine that he had anything to conceal. Ottley and Hankey owed much to Fisher, and he owed much to them, and the nation owes a debt to all three.

Before passing from these reminiscences, I may recall that the anticipation of war filled many of us with apprehension. Not since Waterloo had this country been involved in anything but what may be described as colonial conflicts—Wellington's Army at Waterloo had a strength of only 67,000, of which only 24,000 were British. Since the time of Nelson and Wellington, all the conditions of war had changed: in the Royal Navy the steam engine had replaced sails, the muzzle-loading gun had given place to the long-range breach-loader, the torpedo had appeared. Artillery of unimagined power had been evolved for land fighting. Owing to the *Entente Cordiale* which had been cemented with France, we had accepted military as well as naval commitments, the precise character of which remained unknown.

At this time we were entering, after one hundred years of abstention from war on the grand scale, into a contest of violence far exceeding anything which had been experienced by our forefathers in previous centuries. Some Ministers, a few sailors and soldiers, and fewer civil servants realised the character of the struggle which might lie ahead of us. It seemed to them that we might be driven to abandon our ancient policy of non-military intervention on the Continent, and provide an army on a continental scale. This force, unlike the army of Germany, would have to be transported across the seas and kept supplied with all its requirements by a stream of merchant shipping, the passage of which the enemy would try to stop by every means in his power.

Many of the disciples of the Bluewater school, who foresaw the possibilities which might lie ahead, were filled with dismay and even alarm. Could we bear the strain of commanding the seas against a fleet as strong and efficient as that of Germany, maintaining a vast army on the Continent, and supplying our naval and military forces with food, clothing and munitions? We achieved a miracle, but only because in the years before the opening of hostilities naval and military reforms had been effected in face of much opposition in and out of Parliament, the problems of co-ordinating the national effort had been considered, and the order of procedure had been settled and the plans incorporated in the War Book.

One incident of this period lingers in my memory and, though it belongs to a later time, I may mention it here. Soon after the declaration of war on August 4th, 1914, news came to the *Daily Telegraph* that advance parties of the Army were crossing the English Channel. The idea was scouted; it was impossible. The paper had good sources of information, and it had no inkling of any such step.

I recall the scene in Le Sage's room. None of us would accept the report. I volunteered to obtain confirmation or refutal of the story. I hurried in a cab to the house of a Cabinet Minister whom I knew well. He and one of his colleagues, as well as a group of leaders of the Liberal Party, were about to sit down to dinner. I explained the purpose of my hurried call. I shall never forget the amazement on all their faces. They declared that such an event was impossible. They would have heard of it in the Cabinet.

But it was the fact. The inner Cabinet had taken the responsibility of authorising a step which committed us to a radical departure from the Bluewater policy, which was as old as the Army Annual Act. Each year the British Army, small as it was, had hitherto been preserved from extinction only by the passage of an enabling Act. This had been the sheet anchor of the country's defensive policy. Without knowledge of the Cabinet as a whole, our bluest of blue water policies had been abandoned.

Thus we entered upon over four years of war, in which we lost a million men and won twenty years of unrestful peace. In 1939 we again tried to save France and failed, and were forced by hard circumstances to revert to Bluewater principles. We re-embarked the Expeditionary Force in circumstances which, in the eyes of the future historian, will be regarded as little short of a miracle. When the embarkation took place, the Germans had nearly 1,400 ships, large and small, as targets for attack, and yet 330,000 men were brought back to these shores.

CHAPTER V

"THE McKENNA FLEET"

THE critical phase in the Anglo-German struggle for sea supremacy opened in 1908, when Mr. Reginald McKenna became First Lord of the Admiralty, with Fisher as First Sea Lord.

Though the reform movement had been in progress ever since Fisher had returned to the Admiralty on October 21st, 1904 (Trafalgar Day), this time as First Sea Lord, the votes for the Navy had not been increased. Heavier expenditure had been incurred, but this had been offset by the economies due to the lopping off of the dead branches of the naval tree and by improved administrative measures. The savings thus made, which were used to increase the readiness of the Fleet for war, were the initial triumph of the Fisher régime. It looked as though the country was getting something for nothing. Asquith was Chancellor of the Exchequer, and he met the bills without complaint. Lord Tweedmouth,[1] working quietly at the Admiralty, remained a fairly popular member of the Liberal Party, though a section protested occasionally in the House of Commons and out of it against so much money being spent on the Navy—£34,000,000 to £35,000,000 each year. This money they would have left to fructify in the taxpayer's pocket, or to be used for social reforms which would appeal to the electors.

Asquith, coming straight from the Treasury, became Prime Minister in 1908. It was thought that he would call a halt in "the race of armaments." The economists

[1] Lord Tweedmouth had been Chief Whip of the Liberal Party in the House of Commons.

were further encouraged when Reginald McKenna, a former Financial Secretary to the Treasury (1905–7) was promoted from the Board of Education (1907–8) to be First Lord of the Admiralty. The "Little Navy" group, not negligible in wealth or influence, expected that the Navy Estimates would be drastically reduced. Economy in all departments was to be the order of the day, as they imagined. They did not know the minds of the Prime Minister, his Foreign Secretary (Sir Edward Grey), the Secretary of State for War (Mr. R. B. Haldane), or the First Lord of the Admiralty, or realise their sincere patriotism in deed as well as in thought and word. Probably in the long history of the Liberal Party nothing so disturbing to many of its adherents—especially the more ardent Liberals of "the left wing"—ever occurred as the failure of their statesmen to realise their hopes. Their only consolation lay in the increasingly sympathetic attitude to their point of view of the new Chancellor of the Exchequer, Mr. Lloyd George.

It has always seemed somewhat of a miracle to me that men such as Asquith and his friends, with sound views on defence, especially in relation to the Navy, should have received the support of their party when they formed the backbone of the new Government. The reasonable explanation is that the section of the party which was always demanding the reduction of naval expenditure, without regard to consequences, was smaller in numbers than their vociferous declarations suggested at the time. Asquith had made no secret of his views, neither had Grey nor Haldane. They belonged to the Bluewater school. The Prime Minister when in Opposition some years before had declared:

I need not tell you that the notion that it is needful for us to maintain in this country a huge, unwieldy Army, for the purposes of foreign invasion, is one of the idlest chimeras that ever entered into the brain of man. Why, if you once lost command of the sea, you would be starved into submission before a single foreign soldier had occasion to set his foot upon your shores. What is the moral? The moral, surely, is that, on the one hand, we should watch with the greatest vigilance and jealousy the growth of our military expenditure, and that, particularly after the revelations of the last two years, we should see that we get full value for our money. But, on the other hand, as the Navy is, and must continue to be, the main and ultimate safeguard for our homes and for our commerce, any expenditure is both wise and economical which is needed for the maintenance of our command of the sea.

Grey and Haldane had also openly declared their conviction that the command of the sea must be maintained, whatever the cost.

McKenna became First Lord soon after the revelation that the Emperor William II had written to his predecessor endeavouring, as was suggested, to influence British naval policy. This piece of foolishness on the part of the instigator of German navalism had roused the country. The new First Lord, with his naval advisors, Fisher foremost amongst them, re-examined the position at sea, taking a long-range view. Then came the report that the Germans were accelerating their shipbuilding programme. With the full approval of the Prime Minister, and his chief colleagues, though against the inclination of some of its members—the Navy Estimates introduced on March 16th, 1909, showed an increase of £2,800,000.

Asquith's weakness in surrendering to the "warmongers" was condemned by many of his followers. Efforts were made to organise a revolt in the party, but after the Prime Minister had made one of his most impressive speeches in the House of Commons it fizzled out. But the First Lord of the Admiralty became the most disliked and distrusted member of the Cabinet. It was alleged that he had become the tool of fire-eating admirals, regardless of the need for national economy.

Asquith and McKenna were undismayed by these signs

of revolt. They at least realised the significance of the steps which Germany had taken to increase her fleet by successive Navy Acts in 1898, 1900, 1906 and 1908. In a memorandum published in 1900, it had been stated that "Germany must have a battle fleet so strong that, even for the adversary with the greatest sea power, a war against it would involve such dangers as to imperil its position in the world." The Kaiser had boasted that "Germany's future lies on the seas," and in a flamboyant moment, in order to frighten the people of the United States, he had proclaimed himself "Admiral of the Atlantic." Year by year Germany had replied to every move made by the Admiralty in London with increased financial provision for her fleet; then in 1908 the report reached the Admiralty that the latest programme of construction was being speeded up.

The response by McKenna to this German challenge, when he asked the House of Commons to endorse the Admiralty's larger estimates, convinced a section of the Government's supporters that they had, after all, put their money on the wrong horse; the former Financial Secretary to the Treasury was not running to form. McKenna had the courage to tell the House of Commons that unless his proposals were accepted, Germany might have more battle-ships of the latest type at sea by 1912 than Great Britain would have. The Navy Estimates in those circumstances provided for the laying down immediately of four of these men-of-war, while foreshadowing that four more might be begun before the end of the financial year.

The Opposition raised the cry, "We want eight, and we won't wait!" But the First Lord would not budge, nor did he explain that by the delay of a few months the country would obtain four ships more powerfully armed than if they had been laid down earlier—another surprise for the Germans. In this way the former Radical, who in his younger days had made his mark by baiting the Conservative Ministers with most embarrassing persistency, became the victim of his patriotism. He refused to bow before the storm raised upon the Government and the Opposition benches—one party crying for less expenditure and another for more. He stuck to the policy which had been deliberately adopted as the wisest in the national interests. In fact, in the following July he announced that the Admiralty had decided to proceed with the four "contingent ships"—but even then he could not explain that by the postponement he had achieved two objects. He had given the Germans an opportunity to reduce their programme, and had ensured that better armed ships— "Super-Dreadnoughts" they were popularly called—would be laid down in this country.

The Liberal Party had always voted for the Navy Estimates with regret, and, as a rule, the First Lord in a Liberal Administration was never popular. An exception was Childers, First Lord in Gladstone's first Cabinet of 1868, who saved his political reputation by economies, which eventually cost the country many millions of pounds, exposing it, in the meantime, to great danger. On the other hand, some twenty-five years later, when Admiral Sir Frederick Richards was First Sea Lord and Fisher was Third Sea Lord and Controller of the Navy, Earl Spencer lost the confidence of his party by refusing to cut down his Navy Estimates. The Sea Lords had told Spencer that they would resign in a body unless the Estimates were submitted to the House of Commons. As neither the First Lord nor Richards was good at explanations of policy, this duty fell to Fisher when the defence of the proposals had to be made to the Cabinet; as he put it, he became "Spencer's Aaron." "We got the ships," as he afterwards declared, and for this, among other reasons, Mr. Gladstone, deserted by the majority of his Cabinet on the issue, finally retired from political life. The Liberal Party, until Asquith became Prime Minister, supported by men of equal mind—Edward Grey, Richard Burdon Haldane, Walter Runciman, John Seely and a few others—was never seized with the conviction that for us as islanders everything depends on our being able to live without the threat of invasion and starvation.

As late as 1908 many influential members of the Liberal Party refused to recognise the German menace. The conflict of opinion was so sharply marked that a Liberal M.P. of the Bluewater school issued a warning at this time—"in view," as he stated, "of the activity of a group in the House of Commons, and of statements in the Press as to Liberal policy in regard to the Navy." It was an attempt to educate the rank and file of the party in the essential principles on which the freedom and security of this country and its trade depended. In spite of the expansion of the German Fleet, the caucus known as the National Liberal Federation, which claimed to represent opinion in the constituencies, was unconvinced. McKenna, as First Lord, remained the most unpopular Minister in the Government, for whom M.P.s voted rather than disrupt their party. It was at this period of unpopularity that I got to know the First Lord, and to gain an ever-rising appreciation of his ability, of his stout heart in face of criticism and of his high sense of patriotism.

The partnership of McKenna and Fisher at the Admiralty was an ideal one. The former was the financier and administrator, with a keen eye to economy, and the latter his leading adviser on expert matters. The First Sea Lord was more inclined to interfere in the sphere of the First Lord than was McKenna in that of the expert in naval affairs, but they worked together with a cordiality and loyalty, and even affection, which was probably never equalled at the Admiralty. Fisher's indiscretions, committed in moments of exuberance, must often have been a cause of worry to the First Lord.

McKenna was at the great seaman's right hand when Lord Charles Beresford's long-continued intrigue against the reform movement came to a head in a series of specific allegations against the Admiralty in general, and in particular against Fisher and all that he stood for. Beresford had organised a party of malcontents in the Royal Navy, some of them on the active list, and his following made such an impression on a large number of people that Asquith, the Prime Minister, decided on a formal enquiry, a concession of weakness.

I must make a digression to explain that as a young naval officer, with an Irishman's humour and gift of fluent speech, Beresford had taken a useful part in pleading for a stronger Navy when economy, regardless of consequences, was dictated by a succession of Governments. When still only a lieutenant, he had entered the House of Commons for "the family seat" of Waterford; he had accompanied the Prince of Wales (King Edward VII) on his Indian tour; and in the bombardment of Alexandria had taken his ship, the *Condor,* so close into that port that he had won the signal from the admiral, "Well done, *Condor,*" a message which gained for him promotion from commander to captain. He had afterwards served under Wolseley in the Egyptian campaign. On his return home as a national hero, he re-entered the House of Commons as M.P. for East Marylebone in 1885, and a year later was appointed a Junior Lord of the Admiralty.

If Lord Salisbury thought to silence him by putting him in official harness, he proved to be mistaken. Beresford continued to be a naval agitator in and out of the Admiralty, and in 1888 he resigned as a protest against the Government's niggardly expenditure on the Navy. Thus he once more attracted the limelight. He took to the platform, speaking here, there and everywhere in support of a bigger Navy. He amused as well as interested his audience.

Partly as a result of his action, the Naval Defence Act was passed in 1889, making provision for a large programme of new construction. In spite of his unruliness—for he was the most unruly and, therefore, in the eyes of many people, attractive naval officer of his day—Beresford was afterwards employed at sea. On being promoted to the rank of rear-admiral in 1897, he re-entered Parliament for a couple of years, then went on a mission to China to promote British trade, and again became an M.P. on his return. But shortly after this, he was selected for the command of the Channel Squadron (1903–5), and next he went out to the Mediterranean as second-in-command to Fisher, with whom at first he worked cordially, expressing general agreement with the reforms which he was hatching.

Later his attitude changed. It was alleged by some of his less friendly critics that this change was due to his belief that he, and not his former Commander-in-Chief, should have become Second Sea Lord in 1902.

He was attacking Fisher violently when the choice of a new Commander-in-Chief of the Channel Fleet had to be made, on the retirement of Admiral Sir Arthur Wilson from that position in 1907. Quite incidentally, Fisher mentioned to me that Beresford had been suggested for the vacancy. I agreed that he ought not to be passed over, and that responsibility might curb his activities as the leader of the malcontents in the Navy. In the event, he was given the appointment, was afterwards continually at loggerheads with the Board of Admiralty, and engaged in a fierce quarrel with Percy Scott, who was in command of the Cruiser Squadron under his orders as Commander-in-Chief. Later, when he came ashore, he openly renewed his campaign against the Admiralty.

In these circumstances, my relations with Beresford became less than cordial, because I thought his opposition injurious and doubted the motives which prompted him. At one time, so great had been my admiration of this very Irish admiral that, with his approval, I agreed to a proposal by a publisher to write his life. A contract was signed, but that biography was never written. To many admirers of Beresford, who was a good disciplinarian and popular with the officers and men who served under him, it was a matter of great regret that he should have become the leader of the rebel party in the Navy. At last he formulated definite charges against the Admiralty.

McKenna seemed to welcome the opportunity which the formal enquiry conceded by Asquith gave to him, as First Lord, of exposing the baselessness of the attack. Obtaining a pledge from Fisher that he would remain silent, he conducted the Admiralty case—in a masterly way, I was told by a friend. He had practised at the Bar before he entered the House of Commons, and knew both how to marshal evidence and how to deal with the witnesses on the other side. He gained not only a verdict of not guilty for the Admiralty, but a sharp criticism of Beresford in that he had "failed to appreciate and carry out the instructions of the Board, and to recognise their paramount authority." Fisher resented the weakness of the Government in holding such an enquiry, which he regarded as a reflection upon himself.

In the spring of 1910 the Navy Estimates were again increased, in spite of rumbling murmurs of revolt in the ranks of the Liberal Party. McKenna, who continued to receive the backing of Asquith and the other members of the Cabinet, was unmoved by his own increasing unpopularity. Again in 1911 the Navy votes were for larger sums. The First Lord and the First Sea Lord, grimly determined to pursue their constructional policy, paid no attention to the clamour which assaulted their ears.

Three months before these Estimates were presented to the House of Commons, Fisher, having reorganised the Navy from A to Z and seen the programme of "Dreadnoughts" and "Super-Dreadnoughts" well under way, retired from the Admiralty. He did so a year before he need have done, in order that he might be succeeded by Admiral of the Fleet Sir Arthur Wilson,[1] another strong man as silent as Fisher was loquacious. A great seaman, Wilson was a bachelor who had no other interest in life than the Royal Navy.

[1] Sir Arthur Wilson had been specially promoted to Admiral of the Fleet by an Order in Council in 1907 in recognition of his distinguished services.

RT. HON. WINSTON CHURCHILL,
FIRST LORD OF THE ADMIRALTY—1912

Fisher. 1920

"McKenna's Fleet"

Men-of-War of the Shipbuilding Programmes of 1909–12 and Completed before the End of 1914

(First Lord of the Admiralty, the Right Hon. Reginald McKenna)

Programme	Name	Displacement (tons)	Main Armament	Speed, Knots	
Battleships					
1909/10	Conqueror	22,500	10 13·5-in. 13 4-in.	21	
	Monarch	22,500		21	
	Thunderer	22,500		21	
	Orion	22,500		21	
	Colossus	20,000	10 12-in. 12 4-in.	21	
	Hercules	20,000		21	
1910/11	Audacious	23,000	10 13·5-in. 13 4-in.	21	
	Ajax	23,000		21	
	Centurion	23,000		21	
	King George V	23,000		21	
1911/12	Benbow	25,000	10 13·5-in. 12 6-in.	21	
	Emperor of India	25,000		21	
	Marlborough	25,000		21	
	Iron Duke	25,000		21	
Battle Cruisers					
1909/10	Princess Royal	26,350	8 13·5-in. 16 4-in.	28	
	Lion	26,350		28	
1910/11	Queen Mary	27,000	8 13·5-in. 12 6-in.	30	
	Tiger	28,500		30	
Light Cruisers					
1909/10	Yarmouth	5,250	8 6-in.	25	
	Dartmouth	5,250		25	
	Weymouth	5,250		25	
	Falmouth	5,250		25	
	Blonde	3,350	8 4-in.	25	
	Blanche	3,350		25	
1910/11	Southampton	5,400	8 6-in.	25·5	
	Dublin	5,400		25·5	
	Chatham	5,400		25·5	
	Amphion	3,440	10 4-in.	25	
	Active	3,440		25	
1911/12	Birmingham	5,440	9 6-in.	25·5	
	Lowestoft	5,440		25·5	
	Nottingham	5,440		25·5	
	Fearless	3,440	10 4-in.	25·0	
Destroyers					
1909/10	"H" Class	14,842 (20)*	2 4-in. 2 12-pdr. 3 4-in.	27	
1910/11	"I" Class	17,620 (23)		27	
1911/12	"K" Class	18,946 (20)		32	
Submarines				Surface	Submerged
1909/10	D3–D8	3,720 (6)*	3 T. tubes	15	10
1910/11	E1–E7	4,615 (6)	4 T. tubes	15	10¼
1911/12	E7–E12	4,234 (6)	1 6-pdr. 5 T. tubes	15	10¼

* Figures in parenthesis signify number of vessels.

Summary—18 Dreadnoughts (Battleships and Battle Cruisers)
15 Light Cruisers   63 Destroyers   18 Submarines

I remember two incidents which reveal his character. An explosion occurred during gunnery practice, and a signal came to Wilson, the admiral in command, that several men had been killed. He sent another signal immediately, directing that practice should be resumed. It was the right course, in order that officers and men might not gossip about the sad event and might keep their nerve, but it seemed at the moment unsympathetic and hard-hearted. At another time during manœuvres a dense fog came on. Wilson, with his navigating officer at his side in the flag-ship, would not vary his orders. His Fleet steamed down the Irish Sea at its best speed. I spent a most uncomfortable night in the old tub of a battleship to which I had been consigned as correspondent of the *Daily Telegraph*, got a little sleep, and woke in the morning to find that we had, in the dense fog, entered the difficult waters of St. Mary's, in the Scilly Isles, and had anchored there.

Wilson himself seemed as though he was without nerves. He had no dealings with politicians, much less journalists. The Navy admired him for his very imperturbability, single-mindedness and hardness of heart. He loved the sea and did not covet a chair at the Admiralty; it was only under pressure by McKenna, who gained the ear of King Edward, that he was prevailed upon to succeed Fisher as First Sea Lord. But at last he agreed, content to carry on the work, in all its various aspects, which his predecessor had initiated.

It was about this time that I came across Richard Burdon Haldane, who was Secretary of State for War. While McKenna and Fisher were preparing the Navy for war, he was doing the same work for the Army. Anyone more dissimilar from McKenna, the keen financier with a mind like a razor edge in finding a solution for every problem, and Fisher with his downright, sailor-like way of doing things, it would be difficult to imagine. Haldane was a student, a philosopher and a barrister. He had no belief in such short cuts as Fisher was inclined to take, nor had he any use for the type of business mind that was McKenna's strength.

When he went to the War Office, he found practically everything wrong, except the spirit of the officers and men. The South African War had proved that the military system, based on relief of the Army in India at stated times, could not stand the strain of war. The military organisation was founded on no logical theory in sympathy with the political conditions in Europe. There was a Regular Army, with little idea what its function was, as well as the Militia, and lastly the Volunteers. What exactly these troops, Regular, Militia and Volunteer, were intended to do if the Royal Navy gave the assurance that it could secure command of the sea—and that meant that the country could not be invaded or starved—no one knew. The War Office had carried on from year to year much as in the days of the Duke of Cambridge. As in the case of the Admiralty, old traditions had persisted though all the conditions of war had changed.

Haldane, then in his intellectual prime, sat down to examine all the military problems much as a surgeon examines his patient before operating. He, like Asquith, was of the Bluewater school. Because he was Secretary of State for War he did not, like some of his predecessors, argue that the Army was anything more than the second line of defence; the command of the sea must be the first objective of British policy. He realised that, guarded during transportation overseas by the Fleet, it might become the first line of offence on foreign soil. Haldane's political faith was summed up in the words, "The two things this country most needs are an instructed people and an invincible Navy." He was never President of the Board of Education, which is a pity, but as Secretary for War he held to the belief that the Navy was this country's sure shield.

Haldane came to the conclusion that the Regular Army's main function was duty overseas. It was the projectile to be launched against an enemy with all the swiftness and secrecy that a supreme Fleet could secure. As Fisher for years had been preaching instant readiness of the Navy for war, Haldane took the same text when he went to the War Office. He found that if the War Office were asked to despatch a considerable force to the Continent, it would be unable to do so.

Accepting the naval doctrine whole-heartedly, Haldane determined that the Army needed complete reorganisation. What should he do? He had no doubt as to his first course. It was to study the best organised army in the world, that of Germany. So he went to Germany and examined the German system of military organisation. He realised that he had no occasion to try to equal the German Army in size, and that, in other respects, the British Army's mission, owing to the naval doctrine, was quite dissimilar. He decided that he had to create a striking force, with a civilian army in support of it. Thus the Expeditionary Force came into existence; the Militia disappeared; the Volunteer force, so long the object of derision, was transformed into the workmanlike Territorial Army. A General Staff was created to keep always under consideration how the two armies should be employed in changing eventualities. For the first time in its history, this country obtained a military system suited to its island condition, with a brain. Those were Haldane's achievements, for which he has never received the recognition of his fellow countrymen whom he served with so much devotion.

Throughout this revolution, which met with much bitter criticism in the Army as well as among civilians, the Secretary of State for War had the consistent encouragement of Asquith. The Prime Minister could have vetoed, probably with the support of many members of his Cabinet, all these far-reaching military schemes which meant greatly increased Army Estimates, just as he could have vetoed the reforms in the Navy, which also involved increased expenditure. His party would have applauded him in resisting the movement towards "bloated armaments," in the phrase of the day. As Prime Minister, enjoying great prestige, Asquith thrust aside considerations of party, and with unflinching purpose consistently supported both the Ministers.

When Haldane had organised his General Staff, and had time to look round him and consider the naval side of the problem of defence, he decided that the Admiralty also ought to have a General Staff. What chance was there that he could prevail on the Sea Lords of the Admiralty to set up such a brain? The theory which had prevailed for centuries was that the Sea Lords, in their collective capacity as the Lords Commissioners of the Admiralty, with the First Lord at their head, constituted the brain of the Navy. The admirals when serving at Whitehall had always contended that, with the aid of the Naval Intelligence Department, they were the war planning department of the Royal Navy. No other was needed. Fisher, the most self-reliant of men, was largely in sympathy with this view. He was opposed to a Naval Staff such as Haldane wanted. It was common knowledge that controversy had arisen over this matter. The Admiralty was pulling one way and the War Office, in the person of Haldane and his advisers, was pulling the other.

While this tug of war was in progress, the Secretary for War evidently came to the conclusion that it would be a good thing to get the support of the *Daily Telegraph*. I was asked to lunch at his bachelor home at Queen Anne's Gate. It was the first of many such meals. Though Miss Haldane was present once, we lunched alone. When the meal was over, Haldane invariably led the way to the top of the house, where he had his study. Every inch of space round the walls was occupied by books, many of them in the German language, except for one large cupboard. I recall in particular one of these meetings. As soon as I was seated, he said, "Now, if you have time for a really long talk, we ought to have long cigars." I can see him now, taking his keys out of his pocket, selecting one and opening the cupboard. It was filled with boxes of cigars, reminding me of a report that a former Duke of Devonshire had had a room maintained at a suitable temperature, in which he kept thousands of cigars. Haldane selected a box, and turning to me remarked, "I think this is a suitable cigar for this afternoon. As I am going to talk about the German Army, we cannot do better than smoke one of the cigars given me by the Chief of Staff of the German Army."

Of course, on these occasions I was little more than a listener. Haldane, skilled as a pleader in the Law Courts, explained the advantages of a General Staff adapted to naval conditions with a persuasiveness which it was difficult to resist. As events have since proved, he was right. The Navy needed such "a brain." But at the time the reform was stoutly resisted.

Leading officers, ashore and afloat, were opposed to the establishment of a Naval Staff. At Fisher's suggestion, each Sea Lord had already been given an assistant to relieve him of detail work, and generally the hitherto inadequate *personnel* of the Admiralty had been increased. But Haldane continued to urge reform. So in 1910 the Admiralty, in order to please its critics, announced that in the development of the arrangements for preparation for war, the Naval Intelligence Department had been reorganised, a new department—the Naval Mobilisation Department—being formed, and that a permanent body, termed the Navy War Council, had been established at the Admiralty. The Council would consist of the First Sea Lord as President, the Director of Naval Intelligence, the Director of Naval Mobilisation and the Assistant Secretary of the Admiralty, the latter acting also as Secretary of the Council. The Head of the Naval War College—that also had been one of Fisher's ideas—would attend and act as a member of the Council when the business required his presence. Other responsible officers would be called in to assist and advise when required.

This modest reform was severely criticised. Admiral Sir Cyprian Bridge, who was considered one of the brainiest officers of the Royal Navy, and whose word was regarded by many as final, had been opposed to all Fisher's schemes. In "Brassey's Naval Annual" of 1910 he managed to combine an attack on Fisher with a condemnation of even the modest Naval Council, a good example of his mental agility. When he condescended to treat the matter seriously, he claimed that a navy was so constituted that it contained its General Staff in itself, and consequently did not need an excrescent body to co-ordinate its elements and their efforts. There should, he admitted, be a few assistants to save the chiefs from the work of dealing with details; but those assistants did not, and need not, compose a body to which so sounding a designation as General or Naval War Staff could be properly applied. He contended that the case of an army was altogether different. An army needed a staff, as orders involved the necessity of setting in motion a variety of elements quite independent of each other. But each ship in the Navy had its own staff, and the Admiralty was "the brain of the whole Navy."

He concluded his article by stating that there was unfortunately little hope of convincing those who had succumbed to the General Staff obsession that they were on the wrong tack. "Attempts to adapt it to naval conditions here would be about as hopeful as attempts to acclimatise bananas on the summit of Ben Nevis."

People who of themselves cannot see this will not be made to see it by any power on earth. There are, however, other people who do not necessarily attach magical influence to a mere form of words, or a mere collection of syllables. They know that, no matter what a thing is called, it is likely to be useless, or worse, when out of place. They can understand how mischievous an institution can become when those who belong to it will have little to occupy them except trying to discover methods of making work. They will also know the propensity of officials so circumstanced to form themselves into a class apart, thanking heaven and the new system that they are not as other men are—nor even as are those sea-going officers. This will fix a gulf between the Staff and the Service afloat, that will grow wider at each step from the point of origin. Like everyone else, the Staff officer will expect advancement, and it will be surprising if he does not display great ingenuity in devising means for obtaining it.

But the movement for the creation of a Naval Staff could not be stayed by such criticisms. Haldane, disregarding the conservatism of the Navy, was not discouraged. It is now apparent that he won over the Prime Minister to his way of thinking. It was this cleavage of opinion that at last caused Asquith to decide that Churchill, who had been impressed by Haldane's arguments, should become First Lord, and that McKenna, admirably suited by his legal training for his new post, should replace him at the Home Office. The change-over was a rather mysterious business —a night journey by Haldane to Scotland, where Asquith was staying, and then the dramatic announcement of the change at the Admiralty and the appointment of a Naval Staff.

Looking back on the event, I am satisfied that, if the change of First Lords was not carried out with much tact, it was at least prompted by motives of patriotism. It was in the best interests of the country. My suspicion of Haldane's ideas, as likely to keep too many promising naval officers in Whitehall instead of serving at sea, was weakened as time passed. In writing for the *Daily Telegraph* and the *Fortnightly Review*, I gradually broke away from the attitude of Fisher, because I realised that at some future date we might have a First Sea Lord less competent than he was. I have one letter on this subject which shows that Haldane had a large part in shaping the Naval Staff when McKenna had gone to his new department:

CLOAN,
AUCHTERARDER, N.B.
January 5th, 1912.

DEAR MR. HURD,

It was only this morning that I got from London your article in the *Fortnightly* on National Defence. A more powerful piece of reasoning I have not read. It is admirable—the best exposition of the definite policy that has been decided on after much thought which has yet been laid before the public. The article ought to exercise a powerful influence on the average man, who is the man that counts, and I am glad to see that the newspapers are quoting it extensively. This article is a real service to a great cause.

Very soon you will see the plans for the new Naval War Staff. I have been working at them in close consultation with the Board of Admiralty, and you may assume that they have the entire concurrence of the Army, and are meant to form the basis of close co-operation in the future in the fashioning of a great weapon of Imperial Defence.

We have wholly changed the attitude of the soldier to naval matters. He now accepts the principles which you have explained so definitely.

Yours sincerely,
HALDANE.

During his period of office at the Admiralty, McKenna, besides meeting the expenditure on ships of his predecessors' modest programmes which were advancing towards completion, was responsible for the laying down of eighteen capital ships, fifteen cruisers and sixty destroyers, as well as numerous small craft. It might have been called the "McKenna Fleet," for it was a well-balanced force, complete in every detail. All these ships were completed and at sea before the Great War opened, and were the backbone of the Grand Fleet commanded by his friend, Jellicoe, during the early period of the struggle, which included the Battle of Jutland. If McKenna had shown weakness in face of bitter attack in and out of the House of Commons, or if he had lacked the support of the Prime Minister and the naval programme had been cut down as was urged, with a reduction in the number of officers and men, this country would have been defeated in the Great War. It was "McKenna's Fleet," with a relatively few ships which were laid down in the succeeding twelve months and had been completed by the fateful 4th of August, 1914, that turned the scales against Germany.

After serving as Home Secretary and for two years as Chancellor of the Exchequer, Reginald McKenna gave up politics. A democracy is a hard and often stupid task-master. It frequently judges its servants by false standards. McKenna, who had won success as an oarsman on the Cam and at Henley, and was in every sense a man's man, made more enemies, declared or undeclared, in the House of Commons than friends, owing to his manner. He was a failure as a politician because he would not play to the gallery. Intellectually, he was far above the level of the average M.P.; he had an orderly mind, and had thought out problems to their ultimate issue, especially problems of defence and finance.

At this period in his life he was inclined to be impatient of men of inferior mental calibre, who either could not or would not use whatever brains they possessed. He was said to have " a superior manner." It was almost as though he were guilty of that deadly sin, "the Oxford accent." And thus it came about that as First Lord of the Admiralty, and in a less marked degree as Chancellor of the Exchequer in the years 1915–16, when taxation had to be increased if any considerable part of the war expenditure was to be met out of revenue, he was a rather lonely figure, though he had some staunch friends. As I talked to him, either at the Admiralty or in his home, I came to realise that he was unsuited by his qualities for the rough and tumble of political life. But the gifts of which the nation took little account were afterwards devoted, directly to the management, in particular, of the Midland Bank, and indirectly to the shaping of the country's financial policy.

Since he abandoned politics and left the House of Commons, which has sometimes been derisively called "the talking shop," this former Minister in many offices has made only one speech a year—that delivered to his shareholders.

Haldane fared worse at the hands of his fellow-countrymen. He was the one statesman in history who was ruined by a chance phrase. He had studied in Germany as a young man. He had read widely in German literature. He had seen the German Army at manœuvres, and had talked with its leaders. He had no misconceptions as to the disastrous consequences to both countries of an Anglo-German war. While he worked for the instant readiness of the British fighting forces, he also struggled for peace. In February 1912 he travelled to Germany in secrecy; it was said at the invitation of the Kaiser, whom he had entertained at lunch during His Majesty's visit to London in the previous year. He saw everyone in Berlin of consequence, from the Emperor downwards, and as he spoke German like a native, the conversations were carried on with spontaneity, candour and sincerity.

Progress was, as he afterwards told me, being made to a good understanding on all the outstanding problems, including naval and colonial affairs. Then the Germans, as Asquith afterwards revealed, demanded an absolute pledge of neutrality if Germany were engaged at war. To any proposal which would have left Germany free to do as she liked on the Continent, the Cabinet could make only one reply.

The failure of his mission was the great disappointment of Haldane's life, for he had hoped to become the peacemaker, thus avoiding a war, the consequences of which, in his far-seeing mind, he dreaded. He became the target of gross misrepresentation as soon as knowledge of his mission leaked out. He was assailed as the friend of Germany who could not be trusted by his fellow-countrymen. It was recalled that he had once said that Germany was his "spiritual home."

He had the satisfaction of watching the military machine which he had created work with clocklike precision when the Great War broke out. Owing to his organising genius, this country sent to France a far larger and better-equipped force than it had ever before put into the field. It was a triumph in amphibious warfare. But in the excitement of the moment, little thought was given by his fellow-countrymen to the man who had made it possible. When the first Coalition Government was formed in 1915, Haldane was not among its members. It was apparently considered unwise to oppose popular prejudice, and he disappeared from amongst the front rank statesmen.

As I knew him in after years at the Athenæum, where he sometimes lunched, he was a disappointed and broken man. He had become a peer and had received the Order of Merit, but he had not regained the confidence of the nation. So he occupied his time with such judicial duties as can be carried on by a former Lord Chancellor, in which office he had served after his resignation of the position of Secretary of State for War in favour of Lord Kitchener. He was unique in that he was a great lawyer, a statesman of high achievement and a philosopher of world-wide reputation, but he could never live down the unfortunate confession that his "spiritual home" was Germany.

Haldane, though he successfully adapted the German military organisation to British conditions, McKenna, though he was the creator of "McKenna's Fleet," and Asquith, though he put country before party, were all sacrificed on the altar of an ignorant public opinion, which failed to realise that but for these three statesman, Germany would have won the war of 1914–18.

The fact that the Liberal Party, with its motto of "Peace, Retrenchment and Reform," was responsible for the reorganisation of the fighting Services, and at last declared war on Germany, has seemed to me a providential ordering of affairs. If the Conservative Party had been in office in the fateful years when the Asquith Government was in control of affairs, it would have been harried by the left wing section of the Liberals, and it is unlikely that the Liberal Imperialists, lacking inside information of what Germany was doing, would have given it support. Everyone abroad was familiar with the fine record of the Liberal Party, its devotion to economy and democratic ideals, and its abhorrence of "bloated armaments."

The foundations of our pre-war military policy had been well and truly laid. But what was the course of events in the critical months before we became involved in the war of 1914–18? Without reference to the leaders of naval or shipping opinion, the Foreign Secretary had authorised "talks" between the staffs of the British and French Armies which committed us to a short range military policy with unknown possibilities. The Entente became the Alliance, which implied that we should immediately transport across the English Channel an army on the continental scale. This is what the Germans expected us to do and we lost the main advantage of our sea power, which is to use our limited military strength, as in the Napoleonic Wars, when and where it is most likely to embarrass the enemy, the movement of troops being carried out with that high degree of secrecy which can be obtained at sea.

Thus, without previous consultation with the naval authorities or those who would be responsible for providing tonnage and keeping it efficient under the stress of war, the country was committed to four years of "disappointment and disaster" on the battlefields of France and Belgium, as Mr. Churchill has since admitted, and we became responsible not only for the maintenance of a supreme fleet, an adequate supply of merchant tonnage, and an invincible financial weapon, but of a vast military machine, with its unlimited demand for munitions.

The awakening came in the spring of 1917, when owing to the shortage of merchant ships by reason of the success of U-boats and raiders, we came near to losing the war. The timely intervention of the United States, with its destroyers, saved the situation. The military policy to which the country was committed was far more costly in human life as well as in man power than a Bluewater policy would have been, making sure first of our command of the sea and leaving our diplomats free in the early stages of the war to use our prestige and financial power for the mobilisation of the strength of the threatened countries of Europe for the fighting of rearguard actions, until we were ready to play our full part in the war.

Had the Inner Cabinet determined in the days of acute tension on the war objective which this country should pursue? If so, the decision must have been reached without consultation with the Sea Lords and their experts, the guardians of our sea communications, in face of certain attack by naval forces comparative in strength to those under the White Ensign. The Naval Staff was forced to conclude that the problems associated with the command of the sea, essential to every war effort of an island country, had been put on one side as of secondary importance. The Royal Navy, the Admiralty being the servant of the Cabinet, was committed to the protection of a vast volume of shipping necessary for the transport of the B.E.F., a responsibility which increased from day to day until 2,000,000 soldiers had been landed in France and Belgium, involving the day by day supply of munitions, stores and food.

This dangerous task was imposed on the Royal Navy *before* we had secured command of the sea, for the powerful High Seas Fleet remained undefeated; the vital trial of strength was still to come. The issue of that struggle, which was to test all the empirical theories embodied in our men-of-war, as well as in the courses of training to which the *personnel* had been submitted, might depend on a fog at sea, a few chance hits from enemy guns or torpedoes, or an error of judgment of the Commander-in-Chief of the Grand Fleet or one of his admirals. The one consideration which weighed with the Inner Cabinet was to get the B.E.F. across the English Channel as soon as possible. What the Sea Lords thought of the matter was apparently not considered worthy of a moment's delay.

It is a weakness of our form of Government that in a crisis expert opinion is frequently ignored by Ministers as well as by the Civil Servants, who are more completely the masters of national administration in war than in peace. Political considerations, which are regarded as paramount, too often dominate the minds of Ministers to the exclusion of the lessons of the past and the logical deductions which should be drawn from them. War, after all, is a contest of violence and endurance. As we live on an island, the vital factor is sea power, efficient ships of war and well-manned ships of commerce, and, as a consequence, no major decision on policy—that is, as to the provision and use of the Army—should be decided upon without the advice of the Admiralty and the support of the leaders of the maritime industries, those who build, manage and repair merchant tonnage.

The military policy proved a failure. That is a matter of history. The war resolved itself into a struggle by sea—a war of sea communications. At heavy cost in human life—unnecessarily heavy cost—we managed to keep them open and to close them to the enemy, with the result that, as we became stronger, so the enemy, under the influence of the blockade, became weaker. We won by reason of the resourcefulness of the Admiralty in devising offensive-defensive measures which mastered the U-boat; our superior strength in tonnage, naval and mercantile; and the superior facilities of our shipyards and engine shops, in association with the superior skill of our seamen and craftsmen.

There is a widespread impression that the Americans saved "the shipping front" by the splendid mobilisation and expansion of their shipbuilding resources. That, as the chairman of the United States Maritime Commission has admitted, is an error. The movement began too late. Hundreds of ships were laid down on the other side of the Atlantic, but they were completed too late to take any part

in the war of sea communications. The credit for the final
triumph lay with British shipping and shipbuilding, in
association with the measures adopted by the Admiralty.
Whereas in 1916, owing to the concentration of *material*
and *personnel* on the military effort in accordance with the
Government's policy, the output of the British shipyards was
only just over 600,000 tons, it rose in the following year to.
1,163,000 tons, then advanced to 1,348,000 tons, and in
1919 was 1,620,000 tons—though so much labour and
plant had to be devoted to naval work, for warships of
2,000,000 tons displacement were added to the Royal Navy
during the war in order to ensure, beyond peradventure,
our sea command, the essential foundation of the Allied
victory.

When war broke out in September 1939 we were faced
by naval combinations of much the same character that Sir
Edward Grey in his day had feared, with the added menace
of great aerial armadas. Germany, and eventually Italy,
both reckoned "on paper" as first-class sea powers, were
opposed to us; the French Fleet speedily deserted us; the
Japanese Navy did not support us as in the war of 1914–18,
nor had we even the passive aid of the Russian Navy as we
had in the war of 1914–18. In these circumstances, the two
British Navies of Supply and Defence took up the task of
waging the Battle of the Seas, supported by the workers in
the shipyards and munition factories.

In knowledge of what happened in the war of 1914–18,
as recorded in the official histories of the operations by sea,
land and air, which no Minister in office had probably
read, what should the Government have done when hostilities opened in the autumn of 1939 against a country which
had been arming for three or four years, while we, relying
on the League of Nations, had neglected our fighting forces?
An instructed Government would have copied the Bal-
fournian method and written down on a half-sheet of note-
paper the essential points in the policy of an island country
in their order of importance:

1. Everything depends on command of the sea, and therefore all available and suitable man power must be concentrated on the building of ships, ships of war and ships of commerce, and on manning those ships.

2. Since sea power requires the co-operation of air power, a supreme effort must be made to turn out a large number of aircraft and to train pilots and other *personnel*.

3. When these needs of the sea and the air have been fully met, the Board of Agriculture should be instructed to mobilise the farming industry so as to increase the home production of essential foods.

4. After the foundations of victory have thus been laid, the War Office should increase the Army to a highly mechanised mobile force to be used anywhere as an extension of this country's sea power and air power.

5. Orders in Council should be passed at once, restricting the consumption of all imported goods by the civil population so as to reduce purchases overseas and thus save our shipping for essential cargoes and fortify our exchange, pinning down wages in industry, limiting luxury buying, and in particular,

6. Instructions should be given to the Ministry of Labour to check unnecessary interference by the War Office with the Admiralty, the Ministry of Shipping and the Board of Agriculture, or with the smooth working of the export industries, which can contribute to this country's economic strength.

Under the leadership of President Roosevelt, British Ministers were slowly brought back in the second year of the war to the rightful basis of action of an island power in the twentieth century—first sea command, then air command and afterwards command of the soil as the essential basis of any military operations which might be desirable and possible in later stages of the struggle. The cardinal error of putting the cart before the horse was fortunately exposed before it was too late. For the awakening, this country has to thank in almost equal measure the American President's forthright words and actions, emphasising the supreme importance of the sea affair so that American aid in merchant ships, tanks, aeroplanes and munitions might be effective; and the German High Command, which, by overrunning the countries of Northern Europe drove into our ports 7,000,000 tons gross of merchant shipping and thus averted our defeat. Our deficiency in sea-going tonnage— 2,000,000 tons less than in 1914—was thus more than made good, and we were able to survive the enemy's intensive attack on our life-line in the spring of 1941 while the ship-yards on both sides of the Atlantic, as well as in Australia, were engaged in turning out the men-of-war and merchant ships which, to an island country, dependent for half its food and practically all its war materials on overseas supplies, are the first essentials for victory.

CHAPTER VI

THE CHURCHILL RÉGIME AT THE ADMIRALTY

I HAVE been led away from the chronological order of events, and must return to the measures which were taken to complete our naval preparations before the war clouds burst in August 1914.

That Mr. Winston Churchill, then only thirty-seven years of age and full of vigour and courage, had gone to the Admiralty in 1911 for the specific purpose of setting up a Naval War Staff, whether the Service wanted it or not, soon became apparent. In January 1912 a memorandum was published which bore the impress, in its phrasing, of his strong personality. He challenged the argument that what was necessary for the Army was not necessary for the Navy. In establishing a War Staff for the Navy, the broad differences of character and circumstances which distinguish naval from military problems had to be observed:

War on land varies in every country according to numberless local conditions, and each new theatre, like each separate battlefield, requires a special study. A whole series of intricate arrangements must be thought out and got ready for each particular case; and these are expanded and refined continuously with every increase in the size of the armies, and by every step towards the perfection of military science. The means by which superior forces can be brought to decisive points in good condition and at the right time are no whit less vital, and involve far more elaborate processes, than the strategic choice of those points, or the actual conduct of the fighting.

The sea, on the other hand, is all one, and, though ever changing, always the same. Every ship is self-contained and self-propelled. The problems of transport and supply, the infinite peculiarities of topography which are the increasing study of the General Staffs of Europe, do not affect the Naval Service, except in an occasional and limited degree. The main part of the British Fleet, in sufficient strength to seek a general battle, is always ready to proceed to sea, without any mobilisation of reserves, as soon as steam is raised. Ships or fleets of ships are capable of free and continuous movement for many days and nights together, and travel at least as far in an hour as an army can march in a day. Every vessel is in instant communication with its Fleet and with the Admiralty, and all can be directed from the ports where they are stationed on any sea points chosen for massing by a short and simple order. Unit efficiency—that is to say, the individual fighting power of each vessel—is in the sea service for considerable periods entirely independent of all external arrangements, and unit efficiency at sea, far more even than on land, is the prime and final factor, without which the combinations of strategy and tactics are only the preliminaries of defeat, but with which even faulty dispositions can be swiftly and decisively retrieved. For these and other similar reasons, a Naval War Staff does not require to be designed on the same scale, or in the same form, as the General Staff of the Army.

Naval war, the First Lord added, was at once more simple and more intense than war on land, and he emphasised that the formation of a War Staff did not mean the setting up of new standards of professional merit or the opening of a road of advancement to a different class of officer.

The War Staff is to be the means of preparing and training those officers who arrive, or are likely to arrive, by the excellence of their sea service, at stations of high responsibility, for dealing with the more extended problems which await them there. It is to be the means of sifting, developing and applying the results of history and experience, and of preserving them as a general stock of reasoned opinion available as an aid and as a guide for all who are called upon to determine, in peace or war, the naval policy of the country.

The Staff was to be a brain more comprehensive than that of any single man, however gifted, and tireless and unceasing in its action, applied continuously to the scientific and speculative study of naval strategy and preparation.

With these words, the Naval Staff was introduced. It was to be under the direction of the First Sea Lord, an arrangement that met much of the criticism of the more conservative forces in the Service. It was a radical reform. Years before, Sir James Thursfield had pleaded for "a brain for the Navy," and now that brain had been created under conditions which ensured that it would work smoothly with the Sea Lords, and especially the First Sea Lord.

Lord Fisher, who had been First Sea Lord until January 25th, 1910, and was now in retirement, was an "oil maniac," as his critics described him. Owing to his influence, the first flotilla of oil-fuelled destroyers had been included in the naval programme of 1909, and thenceforward no craft of this type was dependent upon coal. The new First Lord kept constantly in touch with Fisher, and was soon convinced that oil had to replace the solid fuel not only in destroyers, but in all men-of-war. The revolution meant less time spent in port and greater speed at sea, a strategical and tactical advantage.

This change of naval policy involved, of course, problems of supply. As early as 1904 Fisher had investigated this matter when at the Admiralty. He found that limited supplies of oil could be obtained from Burma. The Colonial Office was asked to do what it could to develop the resources of Trinidad, and the Burma Oil Company was urged to help Mr. W. Knox D'Arcy, who had obtained a concession in Persia which, but for prompt action, might have been lost to us. In all these directions, the Board of Admiralty, then under Lord Selborne, had supported the First Sea Lord, and the movement continued when McKenna went to the Admiralty. Indeed, no one could stand against the enthusiasm of Fisher, whose arguments were enforced with all the wealth of language and metaphor which he had at command.

One of Churchill's early acts after taking office as First Lord was to set up a Royal Commission on Oil Fuel and Oil Engines for the Royal Navy, and Fisher was appointed chairman. The report of this body was never published, but the immediate result was a long-term contract with the Anglo-Persian (now the Anglo-Iranian) Oil Company, which assured to the Royal Navy much of the oil that it needed under peace conditions, and provided that the whole of the production would be available to it in time of war. It was also agreed that the British Government should provide a sum of £2,000,000 for further exploration and development.

Churchill, with characteristic courage, carried through all the financial arrangements in the House of Commons under the shadow of what was known as "the Marconi Scandal." His action endangered his political career at a time when, owing to his determination to maintain the supremacy of the Fleet, he had become the target of bitter criticism, and even abuse, by many supporters of the Government. He did not flinch from the ordeal. He claimed that vague insinuations against members of the Cabinet and those in touch with it, such as Lord Murray, should be embodied in definite charges which could be investigated. His boldness in attacking the attackers carried the day. This country acquired a controlling interest in the Anglo-Persian Oil Company.

Thus the constricting influence of the "oil ring" was broken. He also secured for the taxpayers one of the best paying of investments, better even than the shares in the Suez Canal Company. The official reports of the debates in the House of Commons on the proposal are conclusive evidence of the courage which the First Lord exhibited in concluding this far-reaching plan for providing the Royal Navy with oil fuel.

While Churchill was organising the Naval Staff and carrying on the negotiations which were to secure to the Fleet supplies of oil alternative to those provided by the great oil combines, he was giving attention to the possibilities which the conquest of the air now opened up. His imagination was fired, as it had been by the suggestion of higher speeds at sea owing to the adoption of oil fuel. Most naval officers regarded the aeroplane with suspicion as an enemy of the man-of-war; Churchill saw in it an extension of the range and effectiveness of sea power.

The Royal Navy is, fortunately, conservative in its attitude towards everything new and untried. A former Board of Admiralty, consisting of officers of the sail era, had fought the marine steam engine with all its authority, declaring that "they felt it their bounden duty, upon national and professional grounds, to discourage to the utmost of their ability the employment of steam vessels, as they considered that the introduction of steam was calculated to strike a fatal blow to the naval supremacy of the Empire." The statement which had been made when Bleriot first flew the English Channel, that "England is no longer an island," alarmed many senior naval officers. They suggested that the value of naval defence was being restricted. But Churchill realised that air power would develop, whatever might be the attitude of the Admiralty, and came to the conclusion that the Royal Navy ought to have an air arm. So a new department was established at the Admiralty, and in Commander Murray Sueter [1] he secured a proven spirit willing and anxious to study all the problems that the aeroplane had raised in its bearing upon sea power.

As a result of the First Lord's initiative, a Royal Naval Air Force came into existence. As the War Office had been less enterprising in the matter, when the Great War came in the summer of 1914, this force had to be used, not at sea, but on land in support of the British Expeditionary Force. Some years later, in 1916, Balfour declared that the Air Service in the Navy entirely owed its origin to Churchill:

Long before the usefulness of aircraft had been proved
[1] Now Admiral Sir Murray Sueter, M.P.

by experience, he foresaw the important part it was going to play, and set himself to work to lay deep the foundations of a Naval Air Service. He was not content to leave it to others to do, and indeed I suspect that if, in an old-established and traditional office like the Admiralty, this question had been left entirely to what I may call the traditional routine of the office, the Air Service would have made nothing like the progress it did under the fostering care of my Right Honourable friend.

The Naval Air Service afterwards became the nucleus of the Royal Air Force, and it was not until the eve of the war which opened in 1939 that the Royal Navy regained control of its own aeroplanes and pilots, when the Fleet Air Arm was re-established as an essential extension of the power of the Royal Navy for purposes of reconnaissance, gun spotting and other purposes.

But the House of Commons is always more interested in ships than in anything else, because ships cost a lot of money and influence taxation. What M.P.s were anxious to know was, what financial provision for the Navy the new First Lord would propose? He was regarded as an economist, like his father, Lord Randolph Churchill; in former years he had urged the cutting down of the Navy Estimates. McKenna had proved a disappointment to the "Little Navy" section of the Liberal Party. Would Churchill, on succeeding him, fulfil their hopes, now that Fisher was no longer First Sea Lord?

They were not left in doubt for more than a few months. Churchill had inherited from his predecessor a vast ship-building programme, as well as other responsibilities, which meant a further increase of expenditure unless he took drastic measures. He nailed his colours to the mast within a few weeks of his appointment. Haldane was actually in Berlin at the time on his mission of pacification, but Churchill, nevertheless, did not mince his words in a speech he made in February 1912 at Glasgow. He declared that to this country a fleet was a necessity, but to Germany a luxury. The Government, he added, would welcome a friendly arrangement with Germany, but whatever might happen abroad, there would be no whining here, no signals of distress. "The first of all our resources is money, and where the Navy is concerned, we can count upon the ready and spontaneous patriotism of all classes of the population— even the most wealthy." And in a final word, turning to the chairman of the Clyde Navigation Trust, then about to construct a new dock, he exclaimed in a commanding voice, "Build your dock, build it long and build it deep, and above all, build it wide, and we will provide you with no lack of great vessels to fill it."

When the Navy Estimates for 1913–14 were published, they showed that the First Lord had not used such challenging words without the intention of translating them into deeds. The Estimates showed a further rise in expenditure, but after Churchill's speech in the House of Commons in explanation of his policy, no doubts were seriously entertained that the expenditure was essential. He created a sensation by stating that the Two-power Standard, so long the yardstick of the Admiralty, was to be abandoned—had indeed been already abandoned—as unsuited to the new naval conditions when one Navy was racing ahead of all other navies. It was intended to provide instead a 60 per cent. superiority in battleships over the next strongest naval power, which was Germany—the power with practically all her men-of-war concentrated in the North Sea and Baltic. The superiority in cruisers would be 100 per cent. This standard would provide commanding British Fleets in home waters, and leave a margin over for duty in the Mediterranean and the outer seas. At the same time, the First Lord declared that the Government invited Germany to join in "a Naval Holiday" for one year.

It was a cleverly balanced scheme. He urged the House of Commons to agree to a methodical programme for the following six years, so as to maintain a ratio of sixteen to ten in battleships of the "Dreadnought" type over Germany, protesting that in the circumstances this was a policy of moderation in view of the threat to British naval supremacy which the German programme represented. He explained that if additional ships beyond those covered by the current German Navy Act were begun on the other side of the North Sea, he would lay down more ships. In this resolute manner he dealt with Germany's pretensions to command the seas, while at the same time holding out an olive branch. "The time has come," he stated, "when both nations ought to understand, without ill-temper or disguise, what will be the conditions under which naval competition will be carried on during the next few years."

There was, of course, no naval holiday; Germany ignored the invitation. Indeed, a new Navy Act made provision for yet more ships. The 60 per cent. standard of the Admiralty became an 80 per cent. standard, which was, in fact, far higher than the former Two-power Standard, though the First Lord did not tell the Liberal Party that that was the case. Supplementary Estimates were drawn up to counter Germany's new measure, and a further concentration of active forces in home waters was carried out.

It is unnecessary to discuss in detail the courage and ingenuity which Churchill exhibited during his period of office at the Admiralty, when he was assailed from the Government benches for spending too much and by the Opposition for spending too little. He held on his course. The Navy Estimates which were submitted in the spring of 1914 were for no less a sum than £51,550,000. The rebellion in the ranks of the Liberal Party gained strength when it became known that some members of the Cabinet were inclined to resist so heavy a demand on the taxpayers. It was whispered that Mr. Lloyd George, the Chancellor of the Exchequer, had ranged himself definitely against the First Lord. These rumours obtained confirmation when the *Daily Chronicle* published on New Year's Day, 1914, the record of "a conversation" with the Chancellor of the Exchequer. He deplored the cost of armaments, and declared that this was "the most favourable moment which had presented itself for twenty years" of reducing them. "Unless Liberalism," Mr. Lloyd George declared, "seizes the opportunity, it will be false to its noblest traditions, and those who have the conscience of Liberalism in their charge will be written down for all time as having grossly betrayed their trust."

These words were no doubt intended as a warning to the First Lord, but Churchill was undismayed. He submitted his Navy Estimates unaltered to the House of Commons, and only thirty-seven members went into the Lobby against him. His courage was thus rewarded by a remarkable Parliamentary triumph. On August 4th of that year Germany entered upon the war, which lasted upwards of four years, believing to the last moment, before the British ultimatum was delivered, that the British Government would not dare to risk action against so great a fleet as had been built under successive Navy Acts. The Germans had misconceived the character of the Cabinet, with Asquith at its head.

By this time Admiral of the Fleet Sir Arthur Wilson had been replaced as First Sea Lord by Prince Louis of Battenberg, of course, at the instigation of the First Lord, who always chooses his principal naval adviser. Distinguished as had been the services of Prince Louis, the choice was not a happy one for him or for anyone else, as it turned out. Apart from his place of birth—a town in Austria which had been since incorporated in the German Empire —he was well fitted for the position. He knew the German mind as well as the Italian mind. I recall that during "the battle of the standards," when it was being urged that we should build against Italy as well as Germany, since Italy belonged to the Triple Alliance, he told me decisively that it meant unnecessary expense. Italy, dependent upon sea communications in the Mediterranean, which was dominated by the British and French Fleets, would not be so foolish as to come into a war on the side of Germany. She would commit suicide. As events proved, then and in the Second World War, he was right.

And when the crisis occurred in the summer of 1914, he was once more right. The whole British Navy had been mobilised at Spithead in July, had been inspected by King George V and then left for manœuvres. That was the last I saw for three years of what was afterwards to be known as the Grand Fleet.

I went out to Spithead with the Captain of the Fleet, Captain J. E. T. Harper,[1] who had been responsible for the mooring scheme of this vast armada, a most complicated business. We remained off the Nab Lightship while the Fleet passed out to sea in single line. What a sight it was of massive strength! It was intended that, when the manœuvres were over, the ships should return to their home ports and leave be given to the officers and men. But they did not get their leave after all. On July 27th *The Times* published the following announcement:

Orders have been given to the First Fleet, which is concentrated at Portland, not to disperse for manœuvre leave for the present. All the vessels of the Second Fleet are remaining at their home ports in proximity to their balance crews.[2]

The explanation of this dramatic movement was not made known for several months. It was then revealed that at that time the First Lord was spending a well-earned holiday on the north-east coast, having left the Admiralty in charge of the First Sea Lord. On July 23rd Austria had sent her ultimatum to Servia, following upon the murder of the Archduke at Sarajevo. Churchill was disturbed by the possibilities of the situation, and telephoned to Prince Louis. After a short conversation, the First Lord agreed that the First Sea Lord should take any action he considered

[1] Vice-Admiral J. E. T. Harper, Nautical Assessor to the House of Lords; afterwards he was the compiler of the official record of the Battle of Jutland.
[2] "Balance crews" means the officers and men required to place the ship on a war footing.

desirable in the circumstances without consulting him. Thus it came about that no manœuvre leave was given to the crews, and the whole Fleet remained mobilised and ready for any emergency. In complete secrecy, the men-of-war were despatched to their war stations on the night of July 30th, passing through the Straits of Dover northwards. Owing to Prince Louis's prompt action, we won the first trick in the war by sea. We were not caught unprepared, as the Germans had assumed would be the case.

When the Fleet had reached its base in "the Northern mists," Admiral Sir John Jellicoe, the Second Sea Lord, was suddenly despatched from London with a sealed letter to the Commander-in-Chief, Admiral Sir George Callaghan, who was then well advanced in years. That letter contained an order that he was to hand over his command to the younger officer. And thus the last item in Fisher's programme was carried out, and almost on the day he had prophesied, for years before he had declared that the war would not break out until 1914.

Prince Louis's action in the hour of decision did not save him from public obloquy. It was declared that he was a German by birth—which was technically the case—and should not be First Sea Lord. At last he was compelled to bend before the storm, and he resigned. It was a sad business, for a more devoted officer the Royal Navy had never had. Moreover, he had the advantage of possessing an intimate knowledge of the German language, the German mind and German ways. I have never forgotten seeing him for the last time at the Admiralty, after he had decided to retire. Although in ill-health, he bore himself bravely, but he was a broken man. A subsequent First Lord, Lord Lee of Fareham, made the only possible acknowledgment of the cruelty with which he had been treated when he arranged that he should be promoted to the highest rank, that of Admiral of the Fleet.

During those years when Wilson and Prince Louis of Battenberg were filling the office of First Sea Lord, Fisher, who had been raised to the Peerage as Lord Fisher of Kilverstone, was living in a beautiful house just off Ham Common. I saw him frequently, and realised that he was not unconcerned with what was happening in Whitehall. He followed every move with close interest, and I often wondered to what extent he was still a moving force in the development of naval policy. From time to time he went to Kilverstone Hall, near Thetford, which his only son Cecil had inherited from Mr. Josiah Vavasseur in romantic circumstances.[1] One day I received a telegram from him inviting me to go there for the week-end. It was followed by a letter, which I quote because it was so characteristic of the thoroughness with which Fisher did everything, even to looking out trains for his friends.

KILVERSTONE HALL,
THETFORD.

MY DEAR HURD,

     Unexpectedly this morning a spare bedroom turned up here, so I sent you a telegram and I am hoping for a favourable reply. I had my first guests here this week— official ones—arrangements not being possible sooner, and now also the flowers are cut and the grass is growing so it's pleasant here. Please come. No one else here but my family, but all the better for that!

     The 12.20 from St. Pancras is an excellent train and the 9.50 a.m. on Sunday from Liverpool Street. On Sunday to go up if you are obliged to leave 7.9 p.m.—arrive Liverpool Street 9.37.

Ever yours,

F.

29.4.10.

I was tied to London, and telegraphed that I should have to postpone my visit for a day. And then came this second letter:

KILVERSTONE HALL,
THETFORD.

MY DEAR HURD,

     So sorry you can't come till Sunday. You will find my motor waiting for you at Thetford by the 9.50 a.m. from

[1] "Life of Lord Fisher," Volume I, by Admiral Sir Reginald Bacon.

Liverpool St., and I do hope it will be a fine day and that you are able to stay till Monday afternoon. In great haste,

Ever yours,

F.

During this visit I realised more than I had done before what an encyclopædic knowledge of the Bible and Shakespeare this great seaman possessed. In conversation during the week-end, he repeatedly illustrated his points by some apt quotation.

I still have one picture in my mind. I see him walking back from the church at Kilverstone on the Sunday morning of my arrival, in company with Lady Fisher. He looked like the man of the country-side. It seemed incredible that this man of the country-side could have done so much by sea and by land for his country, opposing social and political influences so strong that at times they threatened to overwhelm him. But the strain and stress of life were, as events were to prove, by no means over for his untamable spirit.

Lord Fisher often spoke of the United States during my visit, and it was in that year that his son married a Philadelphian bride. Fisher had a great admiration for the Americans. The future peace of the world, he repeatedly insisted, depended on all the English-speaking peoples pulling together for the maintenance of the ideals, religion and institutions, social and political, which they have in common. He had been in command of the North American and West Indies Squadron years before, and had many friends in the United States. Some months after my visit to Kilverstone he wrote to me:

KILVERSTONE HALL,
THETFORD.

MY BELOVED HURD,

I am just back from America *immensely* impressed by magnitude of *men, things* and *ideas* over there!

I had a tête-à-tête with great men of all walks of life (e.g. the next President, Woodrow Wilson, the President of the Pennsylvanian Railway, who is a huge power, and others of the same calibre). I am assured by them that their present population is over 100 millions now and will be 250 millions!

Their language *English*—their literature *English*—their traditions *English,* and absolutely unknown to themselves and all unconscious of it, their aspirations are English! *We shall be d—d fools if we don't exploit all this!*

I have a great propaganda in view in unison with great men over there, and it *will succeed,* for a great Federation!, but it must be worked with judgment and I will ask for help. I was invited by a mass of multi-millionaires to *"raise the Middle West"* (as they call it) and was assured I would sweep the country just because I gave them a short Royal Academy type of speech! It was lovely! I told them "it was a d—d fine old hen that hatched the American Eagle!" (*That set the oil in a blaze!*), "that George Washington was the greatest Englishman that ever lived, as he taught us how to behave to our children when they were grown up!" *That was an earthquake!* But I won't bore you with more and I've sworn to go back to them all next May!

It was phenomenal the reception they gave me, just simply and solely because I struck the chord of Federation to govern the world. It's a big thing—read John Bright on it!

The real marvel in the United States is the School System. It's a wondrous weapon! No matter what nationalities pour into the country—Germans, Hebrews, Italians, Poles, Irish, Slavs, now in thousands upon thousands, *yet in the second generation they are all pure Americans.* It reminds me of the Chicago sausage! No matter what d—d species of pig goes in at one end of the machine, it's the same identical tasting sausage that comes out at the other end. No trace whatever of the flavour of the original "Porcus"—all blended and assimilated, and hundreds told me with unction that their great-grand-mothers, aunts, first cousins, nephews were English! St. Peter's at Rome will go inside the Central Hall of the Pennsylvanian Railway Station and my son's father-in-law's [1]

[1] The Hon. Cecil Fisher (now Lord Fisher of Kilverstone) married in 1910 the daughter of Mr. Randal Morgan of Philadelphia.

offices are forty stories high and the same ground space as Marshall & Snelgrove, and only clerks in it and every room occupied with safes and lifts, and travelling staircases to the top to conserve energy; and one street at Philadelphia is twelve miles long and three times wider than Regent Street and houses both sides the whole way and I never met one single beggar!

I am coming on December 30th to stay at the Curzon Hotel, Curzon Street, for two months while Sir Hubert Herkomer is painting my picture for Admiralty House, Portsmouth, and then you must come and dine with me and talk over things. Not time for a word more. I've not heard one single word of English news since November 12th, so am absolutely in the dark as to what has happened.

Yours always,
FISHER.
8.12.10.

In the spring of 1912 Fisher went for a holiday on the Continent. While he was at Naples, he was visited by the Prime Minister (Asquith) as well as the First Lord (Churchill). In July he was appointed chairman of the Royal Commission on Oil Fuel and Oil Engines for the Navy. His new task dominated his life. He seemed to have no thought for anything else, but, in fact, he still kept his eye on the Royal Navy, as events were to prove. I saw and heard little of him until he returned to the Admiralty as the successor to Prince Louis of Battenberg as First Sea Lord.

CHAPTER VII

THREE COMMANDING ADMIRALS

THE three admirals who served at sea in the war of 1914–18 in high command, and had the most influence on the course of events, were Admiral of the Fleet Earl Jellicoe, Admiral Sir Reginald Bacon, who held the Straits of Dover against the enemy from the opening of hostilities, and, after Jellicoe had relinquished the command of the Grand Fleet, Admiral of the Fleet Earl Beatty.

Never did a naval officer accept an order more unwillingly than did Jellicoe when he was told that he was to take over the command of the Grand Fleet from Admiral Sir George Callaghan. He had been nominated as Callaghan's second-in-command before the war clouds burst, and was looking forward to serving under that officer. He was busy at the Admiralty on the last days of July 1914, making final preparations for hoisting his flag, when he learnt from the First Lord and the First Sea Lord that, in the event of war breaking out, he might be required immediately to supersede his friend and senior officer, older by seven years. His protests against this decision, as a dangerous one to be taken at such a critical moment, seemed to influence the minds of both Churchill and Prince Louis of Battenberg.

Jellicoe left London for Wick, not knowing the outcome of his strong representations. As soon as he reached his destination, and before leaving for Scapa Flow to join the Fleet, he sent a series of telegrams to the Admiralty. They reiterated his objections to the proposed course in the strongest terms, emphasised the loyalty of the officers and men to the Commander-in-Chief, and even suggested that he should act as his assistant.

As he entered the train in London, an officer from the Admiralty had handed him an envelope marked "secret," which he had put among the other official papers he was taking with him. Early in the morning of August 4th he received a telegram from the Admiralty directing him to open this envelope and carry out the orders specified. He found that, in spite of his repeated telegrams, he had without delay to take over the duties of "Commander-in-Chief of the Grand Fleet," a designation then used for the first time. A similar communication had been made to Callaghan.

It was a most distressing situation for both officers. The senior had had no inkling of the Admiralty's intentions, and the junior had hoped against hope that he would be spared the ordeal of wounding a friend. But both of them bowed to authority, and the sad business of the change over was soon completed. Of Callaghan, Jellicoe afterwards recorded, "He behaved, as always, as a most gallant officer and gentleman, and his one desire was to make the position easy for me, in entire disregard of his own feelings." Thus, in accordance with the plan which Fisher, no longer First Sea Lord, had made several years before, the admiral of his choice was placed in command of the spearhead of the Allied offensive scheme.

Official and unofficial histories of the war by sea have been published. In its documentary aspects, the record has been closed. There is nothing more to be known. There is, however, one consideration which has been too little emphasised—the strength of the German naval forces at the moment when Jellicoe hoisted his flag in the battleship *Iron Duke*. Germany had been building up a great navy for fourteen years, and had spent £300,000,000 upon it. The principle underlying this expansion was that "it is not absolutely necessary that the German Battle Fleet should be as strong as that of the greatest naval power, for a great naval power will not, as a rule, be in a position to concentrate all its striking force against us. But even if it

should succeed in meeting us with considerable superiority
of strength, the defeat of so strong a German Fleet would so
substantially weaken the enemy, that, in spite of the victory
he might have obtained, his own position would no longer
be secured by an adequate fleet."

It was that doctrine which, as Jellicoe realised throughout
his time as Commander-in-Chief of the Grand Fleet, was
being put to a conclusive test. For the Royal Navy had
to maintain the command not of one sea, but of *all* the
seas of the world. Until the Battle of Jutland the issue
was not decided. With the aid of ubiquitous U-boats,
always on the look out for the chance of firing torpedoes,
and mines laid in the track of the Grand Fleet when it was
at sea, the enemy endeavoured, month after month, to
wear down its strength by a process of attrition, persistently
pursued. Throughout the period when Jellicoe was Commander-in-Chief, the enemy hoped by every devilish
stratagem to lure the Grand Fleet to disaster, and his failure
was due to the restraint and skill which Jellicoe exhibited.

The fighting prestige of the German Navy stood high.
When the struggle began, the enemy mobilised a more
powerful and more highly trained fleet than had ever before
challenged this country's supremacy at sea, and all the
conditions of warfare were new—guns of long range, torpedoes of deadly power, aeroplanes with great radius of
action, and airships, as well as mines. The British Navy
had not been engaged in a major action since the era of
sail. Let it not be forgotten in judging subsequent events
that the Germans mobilised on the outbreak of war a fleet
second only to the British Fleet. It consisted of:

Battleships and Battle-cruisers (eighteen of them of the "Dreadnought" design)	40
Coast Defence Ships	8
Big Cruisers	40
Small Cruisers	12
Destroyers and Torpedo Boats	197
Submarines . . . . . . (about)	30

It was a formidable force. In January 1915 the position became critical, because the Germans had ready for action only two fewer "Dreadnoughts" than were with the Grand Fleet, and possessed sixteen pre-"Dreadnoughts" to eight under Jellicoe's flag.

During the Fisher régime I had met Jellicoe casually from time to time, for he was Controller of the Navy for two years before he became, in March 1913, Second Sea Lord, in which capacity he was serving when he was ordered to take over the command of the Grand Fleet. He was the very antithesis of Fisher—a difficult man to know. My appreciation of his wide knowledge of naval affairs as well as of strategy and tactics dates from a winter evening when I was leaving the Admiralty. He was also going out of the building on his way home, and we began to talk as we walked through the park, for he was then living in Sussex Square. We went on and on in the darkness, until he closed the conversation by saying that he would be late for his dinner. By that time I had completely lost my bearings and I was tired, so I found a cab and left the driver to take me back to Fleet Street. That walk occurred many years ago and I made no note of it at the time, but the impression which it left in my mind was such that I have never forgotten it.

Of course, while Jellicoe was Commander-in-Chief "in the Northern Mists" I saw nothing of him; it is a good sea maxim not to speak to the man at the wheel, and I obeyed it. I felt that it would be an impertinence on my part to write to him, though many matters arose during the next two years or so on which I should have liked to have had his views.

Looking back on those months when he was in command of the Grand Fleet, I realise that he was the one man who could have lost the war in a few minutes by one mistaken order. Though he had a large staff, with his brother-in-law, Charles Madden, as its chief, the ultimate responsibility was his, and he was not one to shirk responsibility. He

was, perhaps, too unwilling to share it with officers whom
he knew to be capable, and whom generally he trusted.
His secretary, Paymaster Rear-Admiral Sir Hamnet Share,
told me that when the crisis arose on his meeting the
enemy on May 31st, 1916 (the Battle of Jutland), he was on
the bridge of his flagship. He was an inconspicuous, even
an incongruous figure. He was not in the glory of a commander-in-chief as Nelson was when, with all his orders on
his breast, he fell in with the French Fleet before the Battle
of Trafalgar and walked with Hardy on the quarter-deck
of the *Victory*. Jellicoe was wearing an old burberry over
his uniform, a naval cap which showed signs of hard wear was
on his head and a scarf was wound round his neck, for the
weather was misty and damp.

When he learnt the bearing of the enemy, he walked to
the compass, and, after glancing at the compass card,
instantly gave the order for the deployment of the whole
battle fleet to port so as to form one long line, each ship
in a position to attack the approaching enemy. He sought
no advice from his staff. He knew instantly and instinc-
tively the proper course to take. As has been recalled,[1]
Nelson, with his ships sailing at two knots, had from
two o'clock in the morning until noon on a brilliant
sunny day to decide on the disposition of his fleet for
action. Jellicoe, with his ships moving forward at a rate
ten or more times as great and the weather overcast, had
twenty seconds in which to reach a decision on which not
only the future of the British Empire depended, but the
Allied cause. All the experience of a lifetime devoted to
the study of naval warfare by one of the acutest brains I have
ever come across was concentrated on that decision, which
had to be reached in knowledge that the German commander-in-chief might have a trick up his sleeve to be
played in the gathering darkness.

This was one of the crises of world history. An error of

[1] "Life of John Rushworth, Earl Jellicoe," by Admiral Sir Reginald
Bacon.

judgment while the fleets were approaching each other at a combined speed exceeding that of an ordinary train might have brought the war to an end, for if command of the sea had been lost nothing else would have availed us.

The deployment order was afterwards criticised by men who had never commanded a single battleship, much less a vast fighting organisation such as the Grand Fleet. It should be remembered that in the battle-cruiser action during the early afternoon the Germans had sunk two of our battle-cruisers, under Beatty, and had suffered only slight damage. The news of these successes was signalled throughout the High Seas Fleet; so a spirit of elation, confidence and daring had been created. The Germans believed that their initial success was an augury of a greater triumph when they should fall in with the battle squadrons under Jellicoe. *Deutschland Uber Alles!*

Admiral Scheer throughout the action proved himself a most capable commander, and one unlikely to let an opportunity slip by. If, as has been suggested, Jellicoe had deployed on the "Marlborough" Division (i.e. to the starboard), Admiral Scheer would have found himself across the "T" of the Division, and would have made the most of the situation. For a quarter of an hour or more the last three columns of the Grand Fleet would have been exposed to a superior gunfire at ranges from 8,000 to 12,000 yards, and so bunched up would have been the half of our battle fleet that in a successful torpedo attack there would have been about an even chance of some torpedoes hitting a battleship, instead of a two to three chance as against ships in a normal line ahead formation.

That the Germans escaped annihilation, it is now known, was due to a regrettable error at the Admiralty, as was revealed when a revised edition was published of Volume III of the late Sir Julian Corbett's "Naval Operations," the official history of the naval war of 1914–18. In the preface Lieut.-Colonel E. Y. Daniel, Secretary of the Historical Section of the Committee of Imperial Defence, explained that every endeavour had been made to preserve the work of the author, and that no disturbance had been made except where essential for historical accuracy. But he had added an appendix, giving a list of seven German signals received and decoded by the Admiralty between 11.15 p.m. on May 31st, 1916, and 1.25 a.m. on the following day. Each message contained the news that the German High Seas Fleet was proceeding home via the Horns Reef Passage, and in one of them, by some mischance, four vital words were omitted from the decipher which Jellicoe received. This signal was: "Be assembled by 4 a.m. *with own main body* at Horns Reef, or course round Skaw." In deciphering the message the italicised words were omitted, and Colonel Daniel's comment is: "Had the officer responsible for the deciphering of this message realised the vital importance of the information it conveyed, it is hardly to be credited that it would have been withheld from Admiral Jellicoe." The Commander-in-Chief, in fact, did not receive until 4.15 p.m. on June 1st "a startling message from the Admiralty" to say that at 2.30 the German main fleet was in a position only sixteen miles from Horns Reef light vessel, steering south-east by south at sixteen knots. Then only Jellicoe realised that the enemy had effected his escape; eight hours after the German Fleet reached Horns Reef he was still at sea, hoping that the enemy would resume the battle.

I knew little of what happened at the Battle of Jutland beyond what was published in the newspapers until several months later, when Jellicoe hauled down his flag for the last time and became First Sea Lord, in succession to Admiral Sir Henry Jackson. In spite of the claims of the enemy and the criticisms of irresponsible and ill-informed critics among his own countrymen, Jellicoe knew that the German Fleet, defeated though not annihilated, would never again stand up to the Grand Fleet in a battle action. In the following months, he continued his watch and ward, but his thoughts were turned to the increasing losses of merchant tonnage owing to the operations of the U-boats. The enemy, his hopes frustrated of winning command of the sea, had turned to an intensive submarine campaign. Every consideration of law and humanity was cast to the winds. By every means at his command, merchant ships, British, Allied and neutral, were attacked. It was evident that the Admiralty had been caught unprepared for such a development.

From the time when the German High Seas Fleet had been defeated, the losses of tonnage (British, Allied and neutral) steadily rose. In June, they were 108,000 tons gross, but in September they exceeded 230,000 tons, in the following month they were 353,000 tons, and in November 311,000 tons. Jellicoe's anxiety found expression in letters to the Admiralty; he even suggested that he could spare ships from his command to assist in hunting down submarines. On October 29th, 1916, he wrote:

There appears to be a serious danger that our losses in merchant ships, combined with the losses in neutral merchant ships, may by the early summer of 1917 have such a serious effect upon the import of food and other necessaries into the Allied countries as to force us into accepting peace terms which the military position on the Continent would not justify, and which would fall far short of our desires.

In this letter he discussed the problem at length. He was afterwards asked to meet the War Cabinet, when he pressed for the appointment of a committee of young officers with expert knowledge and ideas. A conference at the Admiralty followed. Jellicoe's suggestion was approved. And then came a surprise—and one that was on personal grounds unwelcome. Balfour, who was then First Lord of the Admiralty, suggested to him that he should come to London and tackle the problem himself, forming a new department at the Admiralty. Jellicoe came to the conclusion that the arrangement would not be satisfactory.

At last he was urged to become First Sea Lord, and, moved by anxiety to serve the nation in its hour of ordeal, he reluctantly accepted this office at a moment when the whole Allied cause depended on the discovery of new methods for meeting the enemy's attack.

The Board of Admiralty was reconstituted, with Sir Edward Carson as First Lord, and Jellicoe set to work, fully realising that immediate results were not to be expected. First of all, the enemy's tactics had to be carefully examined, and then means evolved for countering them. A new division of the Naval Staff, under Admiral Sir Alexander Duff, was established. Plans of action were forthwith prepared and orders for new devices were given— hydrophones and other gear, more "Q" ships, depth charges, flotillas of high-speed motor-boats, smoke apparatus, a new type of mine. None of these measures could reach fruition for many months, for they involved large-scale manufacture.

The losses of tonnage continued to rise month by month. Jellicoe did not conceal his anxiety from the War Cabinet, presided over by Lloyd George, the optimist who had from the time when he became Prime Minister been the despair of everyone with technical knowledge. He could not or would not understand that the U-boat peril was not to be mastered by waving a wand or making a speech. He was impatient of delay. He wanted immediate results, and cheerful assurances that all would be well. Jellicoe refused to cheer him up, and so he decided that Jellicoe must go.

Of all incidents in the history of this country since Ministers were despatched by despotic kings, the dismissal of Jellicoe from the Admiralty by Lloyd George, at the instigation or with the concurrence of Eric Geddes, who had become First Lord when Carson had been got rid of, was the most disgraceful. Geddes was a railway man, and as such had been successful, both in this country in peace and in France during the war. He himself was doubtful of his fitness for the high and responsible office of First Lord of the Admiralty, when it was pressed on him by the Prime

Minister, but on Jellicoe trustfully promising him support he accepted it. He was a man after Lloyd George's heart—cheerful, confident, always in a hurry to produce results. No men more ignorant of naval affairs were ever associated together than the Prime Minister and Geddes. It was said of Beresford by Winston Churchill, in one of his happiest moments when Beresford was attacking Fisher, that when he got up to speak he did not know what he was going to say, that when he was on his feet he did not know what he was saying, and that when he sat down he did not know what he had said. Lloyd George was a speaker of a different type, but quite as irresponsible. To an East End audience of have-nots he would deliver a Limehouse speech, but in the West End his utterances were such as a duke could applaud. In the days before the war he drew his inspiration from his audience. He was well fitted to become the hero of a democracy when at war—the man in the street nervy, doubtful and over-anxious for speedy victory.

He brought to his office of Prime Minister fiery eloquence, charm of manner and superhuman energy. These qualities were associated with contempt for the expert. He believed that any problem could be solved at once if the will to do so were there, even though he was told by men with knowledge and experience that, if a solution was possible, it would necessarily be a matter of time, skilled labour and suitable material. I have since thought that "L. G." must often have been impatient of the processes of nature since, in later years, he took up farming in Surrey. How he must have reviled the slowness of spring, when great chemical processes are going on out of sight, the apparent lack of progress in the warm, sleepy days of summer and the tardiness in the autumn with which fruit ripens, the corn becomes golden and the good soil at last yields its increase. He probably believes that God did, in plain fact, create the world in six days and rested on the seventh.

So Lloyd George was impatient when Jellicoe and his

staff failed to develop immediately successful counter-measures to the German U-boats, which were ignoring all the laws of God and man in pursuit of their sink at sight policy, a development which, before Jellicoe went to the Admiralty, had defeated the Sea Lords and their advisers. In November 1916—that is, before Jellicoe was recalled to Whitehall—the Board of Admiralty had prepared a memorandum for the War Council in which the following statement was made:

Of all the problems which the Admiralty have to consider, no doubt the most formidable and most embarrassing is that raised by the submarine attack on merchant ships. No conclusive answer has yet been found for this form of warfare, perhaps no conclusive answer will be found. We must be content with palliatives.[1]

Lloyd George had been described by flatterers as a wizard, and Jellicoe's methods were not those of a wizard. On the contrary, he and the officers at the Admiralty whom he gathered round him, and notably Admiral Sir Alexander Duff, first studied the problem with the aid of the best brains of the whole Navy, and then, when decisions had been reached, they gave orders on a vast scale to industry, knowing that, however whole-heartedly masters and men might work, time would elapse before the goods could be delivered. In the meantime, the First Sea Lord continued to remind Ministers of the gravity of the situation. He would not even promise a complete and speedy reply to the German attack. He would merely promise that everything humanly possible would be done to master the submarine, as well as to deal with the menace of the mine.

But this was not enough for the Prime Minister, nor did it satisfy Eric Geddes. They knew better than the experts, and so, on December 27th, 1917, Jellicoe was dismissed with a discourtesy without parallel in the dealings of Ministers with

[1] When those words were written, Admiral Sir Henry Jackson, the most scientifically minded officer in the Royal Navy, was First Sea Lord.

distinguished sailors and soldiers. This bombshell was exploded when, as the official record of the orders given by him shows, he had laid the foundation of victory over the U-boats, for which Lloyd George and Eric Geddes received the credit.

I became aware of this explosion when I called at Mall House, then the official residence of the First Sea Lord, on the afternoon that Jellicoe had received his congé in a curt note from Geddes. The First Sea Lord was in the drawing-room. In the centre of the room stood a beautifully wrought model in silver of the battleship *Iron Duke*, which had been his flagship as Commander-in-Chief of the Grand Fleet. This gift of affection had just been made to the First Sea Lord by the captains who had served under him, and had come to love him. A representative group had visited Mall House to make the presentation, and they had just left when the dismissal was placed in Jellicoe's hand.

Let it be emphasised that Jellicoe had given up his command at sea unwillingly under pressure from Balfour. He was satisfied that the Fleet which he had inherited, and by his genius of organisation and command had transformed into a supreme instrument of war, would not again have an opportunity of meeting the enemy. The Battle of Jutland had settled the account with the High Seas Fleet. No further Fleet action was to be expected.

That was all the more reason why Jellicoe, having spent many days and nights in anxious thinking and planning to create the Grand Fleet, might have desired to retain his command. But when Balfour represented to him that, owing to the success of the enemy's U-boats in sinking merchant tonnage, this country was in danger of starvation and the Allied cause of overwhelming defeat, Jellicoe gave way. He was moved to this surrender by as lofty a patriotism as led Nelson to give up his life for his country. Thus, having made this sacrifice and accepted office at the Admiralty in order to carry out a task which seemed to many naval officers an impossible one, he was summarily dismissed by the man who, as a young Welsh attorney, had managed to captivate the imagination of the English people by his eloquence, his gestures and his courage, for in the darkest days of the war Lloyd George showed the supreme quality of courage.

So the great naval leader, when he had set in motion the forces which eventually mastered the U-boat, was dismissed much as though he had been an unsatisfactory butler—and without a character. The story is told that after the war, when the list of honours to the leaders by sea and by land was forwarded by the Prime Minister to King George V, Beatty was recommended for an earldom and Jellicoe only for a barony. It is said that His Majesty—who had served in the Royal Navy for many years and appreciated the significance of the events which had occurred at sea—demurred to the indignity which such a meagre reward to a great sailor would imply in the eyes of his fellow-countrymen, and that by way of compromise Jellicoe was made a viscount. It should be added that on the earliest opportunity after Lloyd George had left office, Jellicoe was given a further step in the Peerage and became Earl Jellicoe.

After his dismissal Jellicoe would never discuss the matter; he would merely shrug his shoulders. Such friends as Asquith, McKenna, Carson and Runciman wanted to extract a justification for the Prime Minister's action, but the country was at war and it was no time to pursue the matter. Jellicoe lived to be acclaimed by his fellow-countrymen as the outstanding hero of the naval war.

There was nothing heroic about his appearance or his manner, and though he wrote quickly and precisely, he was not, like Beatty, an effective public speaker. He was small in stature, had none of the swagger of the stage naval officer, and hated publicity of any kind. He had, in fact, none of the outward signs of the popular hero, but whatever he did, whether it were shooting, fishing or golfing, running a department at the Admiralty or commanding a squadron or fleet at sea, he did it well. In his home he was the perfect husband, father and friend, and the leader in the domestic circle. I remember a Sunday morning when breakfast was over, and he and his family and guests were dispersing. "I don't know what the rest of you may care to do," he said, "but I shall go to church." A strict disciplinarian at sea, he led by his example rather than by command.

He was essentially a good man, who gained friendship by no meticulous appeals to popularity. He disliked anything sordid. I recall that when he, at length, reluctantly agreed to write the first of his books, "The Grand Fleet," and did so on the understanding that I would give him what aid I could, he remarked that such co-operation would take up my time, and the labourer was worthy of his hire. But he felt a delicacy in making any overtures, and suggested that I should talk the matter over with his cousin, Eustace Burrows, who was secretary to the Great Northern Railway. So I talked with Burrows in his room at King's Cross. He made suggestions which I accepted. And the matter was never afterwards even mentioned by Jellicoe.

He served as Governor-General of New Zealand. It was a singularly happy period of his life. He and Lady Jellicoe became the friends of the people of the Dominion, and spared no effort to promote their interests. It was hard work, but there were many compensations. I corresponded with Jellicoe regularly on matters of common interest, for at the time I was engaged on the official history of the part which the Merchant Navy had taken in the war, and the Governor-General, himself the son of a merchant officer, was keenly interested in justice being done to the merchant seamen.

The second commanding admiral during the war, using that adjective in its full meaning, was Admiral Sir Reginald Bacon. He shared Jellicoe's martyrdom, and was dismissed about the same time, after he had developed the defences of the Straits of Dover with such conspicuous success that the transport of troop and store ships across the English

Channel was carried out without the loss of a single life—an unparalleled achievement in naval history.

I was lunching with Jellicoe at the Bath Club, when a messenger stated that Admiral Bacon had called to see him. He was absent for a quarter of an hour or so, and then told me that Bacon had called to consult him about a book he was writing on the Dover Patrol. He had asked Jellicoe to suggest someone who would help him in getting the volume into shape. Thus I came to be associated in a very unimportant way (for Bacon proved himself a most effective writer) with the three volumes which were subsequently published.

Throughout his career Bacon had been known as the officer to whom a task requiring energy and brain could safely be entrusted. He had taken over the first submarine to be built in this country, and subsequently became the first officer commanding the submarine branch of the Navy. He was the first captain of the first "Dreadnought."

When the war broke out and defences had to be devised for the Straits of Dover, Bacon was selected for the task because he had a scientific mind, was not afraid of difficulties and was, above all, a seaman of infinite resource. He had acted as managing director of the Coventry Ordnance Works since his retirement from the active list, after serving as Director of Naval Ordnance at the Admiralty, so he had first-hand and recent knowledge of material and what could be done with it. He had designed in the early days of the war a 15-in. howitzer which could be transported by road. I am not qualified to explain how he performed this miracle, but he did perform it. The War Office had refused to have anything to do with this novel development, but Winston Churchill, then at the Admiralty, had been less conservative, so twelve of these guns were manufactured.

He was obviously well fitted to undertake the difficult task of closing the Straits of Dover against the enemy. He accepted this duty at a time when Ministers did not realise its importance, and when steel and labour were in short supply. Any system of defence involved material and labour. His success was not a matter of opinion, but of results which were capable of statistical proof. But he had not the mind or manner which appealed to a man of Lloyd George's temperament.

He had spent his life in the study of his profession in all its aspects. His mind was stored with exact knowledge, whereas Lloyd George had essentially an untutored mind. Moreover, he was not a man of glib speech and dramatic action, who boasted of what he would do. Bacon was still building up the defence system in the Straits, which involved material such as nets and mines which were not to be obtained rapidly, when he was summarily dismissed from his command by Geddes, the First Lord. Of his removal Bacon did not complain, because, in war especially, the Board of Admiralty is supreme.

But in my removal and afterwards, the Board of Admiralty then in office did everything in their power to make my removal as bitter to me as possible. It is usual after an officer has vacated a high command for him to be received by the First Lord and thanked for his services. I was not favoured with such an interview. It was also the established practice of the Admiralty under these conditions to write to the Admiral expressing their appreciation of his services. This letter in itself means little; but its omission means a great deal. This letter was never sent. Again, under these conditions, it is usual for the Admiralty to ask His Majesty graciously to receive an officer vacating a high command. As this was not done, I suggested that the omission should be rectified. I was told that the Admiralty did not intend to do so.[1]

As in the case of Jellicoe, this distinguished officer, who had given his life to his country, was treated with the utmost discourtesy. But in retirement he has since related

[1] "From 1900 Onward," by Admiral Sir Reginald Bacon, K.C.B., K.C.V.O., D.S.O.

10

the story of his triumph over the perils of the sea and
the wiles of the enemy during the period when he was
Admiral-in-Command at Dover. It was not the kind of
wizardry to appeal to Lloyd George, because it involved
the application of exact knowledge acquired during a long
lifetime of naval service.

But the admiral indulged in no lamentations. In his
country house in Hampshire, he fell back on his resources
of brain and hand—writing books, carpentering, working in
iron with a deftness I have never known excelled, rigging
models of sailing ships, and so on. After such a life as he
had led and with his abilities, he could not be idle; he did,
however, find time to act as chairman of the local bench and
do other public work.

The third commanding admiral of the war who has left
his mark on the history of that ordeal is Beatty. I suppose
he was the handsomest officer of his day, always spick and
span whether in uniform or in mufti and with his hat
worn at an angle which suggested a devil-may-care attitude
to life. He had a dashing manner, reminiscent of Terriss
on the stage of the old Adelphi Theatre when he was
playing the part of a naval officer. He was well known in
the shires as a daring rider to hounds, and he brought the
same spirit to any naval task that was entrusted to him.

It was impossible not to admire him. He somewhat
resembled Beresford, but had a better brain, and he possessed a rare gift of selecting the right officers to serve under
him, whether at sea or at the Admiralty; men of ability
who thought and planned and worked, while he exercised
a general supervision over their activities. That is no mean
gift in an admiral. Beatty was a supreme leader of men.
He looked the part—that of an admiral of the Royal Navy.
Moreover, he was an effective speaker, whether on his
quarter-deck, at a public meeting or, so I have been told,
in the Cabinet when, at the end of his active career, he
became First Sea Lord. He knew what he intended to say
and said it, tersely and crisply in a commanding voice.

He did good service after his active career was at an end
in reminding the nation of the folly of cutting down the
Navy. I had the privilege at a dinner of proposing the
toast of his health, and I still remember the change in the
attitude of the gathering when I sat down and he rose to
reply. Everyone bent forward to catch every word that he
uttered.

After the opening of hostilities in August, 1914, I saw
nothing of him, until the autumn of 1918. I had been
so busy in London that I had never visited the Grand Fleet,
either while Jellicoe was Commander-in-Chief or afterwards
when Beatty had succeeded him. I was talking to the Chief
Naval Censor at the Admiralty when the omission was
mentioned. Admiral Sir Arthur Leveson, then, as at the
Battle of Jutland, in command of the 5th Battle Squadron,
sailed into the room like a three-decker battleship. He and
I had been friends for some time. He suggested that the
Chief Naval Censor, who arranged visits to the Grand
Fleet, should send me as his guest on board his flagship,
the *Barham*.

So it was arranged that I should spend a week or so with
him, and see what was going on. I shall never forget those
days, for Leveson was an ideal host. We called on many
of his friends in other ships, and I had a very good time.
But the memory which I retain most vividly is of my "duty
call" on the Commander-in-Chief. When we reached the
battleship *Queen Elizabeth*, we passed into an ante-room to
the Commander-in-Chief's quarters, where his staff, all first-
class men, were gathered. Then we were ushered in to
Beatty, of course in uniform. He was no longer the young
officer attending on even so important a person as the
First Lord of the Admiralty, as I had seen him when
we had last met. He was the Commander-in-Chief, and
he bore himself as such, talking pleasantly, but as one
accustomed to give orders and to be obeyed—at the double.
I came away deeply impressed with his personality.

When the Jellicoe–Beatty controversy arose over the

manner in which the Battle of Jutland had been fought, I realised the essential difference in the characters of the two officers—the one the student of naval warfare who had been Controller of the Navy and Second Sea Lord at the Admiralty, weighing with a broad mind the pros and cons of his every act, the other a man of high spirit, who was always willing to take a chance, whether on the hunting field or at sea.   My faith in Jellicoe's wisdom was confirmed by my visit to the *Queen Elizabeth*.   When the fate of the Allied cause was at stake, and the future of the British Empire hung on a single order given after a few seconds' consideration, I had no doubt which was the man in whom to place confidence.   As a layman I resented the suggestion, from whatever quarter it came, that Jellicoe had been nervous and timid, intent only on preserving his ships. As I came to know him, he was as determined as was Beatty, but he never failed to weigh the possible issue of his every act.

Who was responsible for the campaign against Jellicoe for his handling of the Grand Fleet at Jutland?   The outstanding figure was Arthur Hungerford Pollen, who wrote on naval events in the war in *Land and Water,* now dead. He was an eloquent talker and a good writer, and had an expert knowledge of gunnery.   I recall that one day when Leveson and I were lunching at the Savage Club, in its old quarters in the Adelphi, we met Pollen, who seized the opportunity, he being a landsman, to tell the admiral in command of the 5th Battle Squadron how the action should have been fought.   He talked and talked and talked, and Leveson remained attentive, but silent, seemingly impressed. At last Pollen made a statement which drew fire.   Leveson almost shouted, "I tell you we went for the Germans like hell for leather, and that is the end of the matter."   And it was the end of the matter, for he and I left the club.

The injustice which was done to Jellicoe was short-lived. But I have never understood why or how, while the war was still in progress and the Germans were lapping up every word of the attack, such a movement could be carried on by patriotic men. It was based on misstatements and miscalculations. History will obliterate the last traces of an ignoble agitation, and future generations as they visit St. Paul's will honour the man who, in the hour of its greatest peril, saved this country and the British Empire.

CHAPTER VIII

THE DISASTER OF THE DARDANELLES

LORD FISHER was recalled to the Admiralty on October 30th, 1914, to succeed Prince Louis of Battenberg as First Sea Lord, within a few days after the country had been dismayed by the news of the disaster to Admiral Cradock's weak squadron off Coronel.

In order to appreciate his resignation of that office in the following May, it must be borne in mind that throughout the interval between his retirement from the Admiralty early in 1910 and his recall, he had exercised a great influence on Winston Churchill, though he had resented the manner in which Mr. McKenna had been transferred from the Admiralty to the Home Office, and disapproved of the form which the Naval War Staff had taken.

As a matter of patriotism and personal satisfaction, he was anxious that the schemes he had initiated and on which he had worked with such vigour should not be jeopardised by any action by his successors in office, or by the impetuous and strong-willed First Lord, who had made himself master of the Admiralty. So he and the First Lord were repeatedly in consultation, even though he was nominally investigating the possibilities of oil fuel, as chairman of the Royal Commission which was set up in July 1912. When the agitation against Prince Louis as First Sea Lord caused that officer's resignation, Churchill decided that his successor should be Fisher. But for the First Lord's insistence, the appointment would never have been made.

Fisher had wanted nothing so much as to get back to the

Admiralty. Thus he returned with the feeling that he had to thank the First Lord for the opportunity of super-intending the working, under war conditions, of the New Navy which he had created. That sense of obligation over-shadowed him in subsequent months; he was anxious, however great the strain, to repay by loyal co-operation the service which Churchill had rendered him in giving him his chance.

The partnership opened propitiously. On news reach-ing the Admiralty of the Coronel disaster, Fisher decided that the defeat must be wiped out. He gave orders that the battle-cruisers *Invincible* and *Inflexible* were to be instantly withdrawn from the Grand Fleet and despatched to waylay Von Spec's squadron. He would brook no delay; every plea that these men-of-war could not be ready for some time owing to defects was swept aside; they were to put to sea on the day he had selected; if any man stood in his way, he would make his wife a widow and his home a dunghill! When they sailed, some of the contractors' staff engaged on the electrical equipment sailed with them, and thus these civilians were spectators of the Battle of the Falkland Islands.

Nothing in his later years gave Fisher greater satisfaction than the result of this action. It came as a tonic to the nation, and raised the prestige of the Royal Navy to a point which had not previously been touched since the war had begun. Fisher's pride in the battle was dominated by the fact that he was the creator of the battle-cruiser type of ship which had destroyed Von Spee's squadron. He regarded it as the greatest triumph of his life. When his volume of reminiscences, which he entitled "Records," [1] was published in 1919, he sent me a copy, and on the fly-leaf was inscribed, in his masterful handwriting, words giving a summary of the battle and its results:

,

[1] Lord Fisher sent me his companion volume, "Memories," with the inscription, "From his ever grateful friend, Fisher, 21 October, 1919 (Trafalgar Day). 'There is a friend that sticketh closer than a brother.'— Proverbs 18, verse 24."

FISHER
Admiral of the Fleet
December 8, 1919

Being the Anniversary of the Annihilation of Admiral von Spee's Squadron, whereby nitrates came to England to enable our munitions to be produced—Africa was saved—and a second Heligoland avoided at the Falkland Islands, and our Commerce saved in the Southern Oceans. The Dreadnought battle-cruiser that sank Admiral von Spee had not a man killed or wounded! Yet I do not turn and rend my detractors. I leave them one and all to "the worm that gnaweth"!

It was a tragic business that this swift assertion of the power of the New Navy, which reflected, of course, on the First Lord as head of the Admiralty as well as on the First Sea Lord, to whose genius it was due, should have been followed by a period of increasingly strained relations in the everyday work of the Admiralty. The whole story has been told by the First Lord in "The World Crisis" from his point of view, and by Admiral Sir Reginald Bacon from that of the First Sea Lord. It culminated in Fisher's resignation over the Dardanelles Expedition, the disappearance of the First Lord from the Admiralty and the formation of the first Coalition Government.

When Le Sage heard at the *Daily Telegraph* office that Fisher had resigned and the dramatic manner in which he had absented himself from the Admiralty without a word to anyone, he remarked, "That is unforgivable. No officer in a highly responsible position has the right to resign his appointment in time of war. A personal quarrel, whatever its cause, is no excuse when the country's safety, and that of the whole Allied cause, is in danger. His duty is to his King and country." When it became known that Fisher, on being urged by Asquith to withdraw his resignation, had delivered an ultimatum containing stiff terms, Le Sage, who had always supported Fisher through thick and thin, even when the agitation against him had been most widespread and fierce, reaffirmed that he had committed the unforgivable sin in any officer in time of war. He had always applauded Sea Lords who, in peace time, had threatened to resign rather than permit the Navy to be reduced below what they regarded as the safety standard, but the condition of war, in his opinion, made all the difference.

During the storm Fisher was lost to the world. It was said that he had gone to an unknown destination in Scotland, but he remained, in fact, for a few days in London before he finally disappeared, refusing to have any communication with his friends.

The tragedy of the Dardanelles is now an old story, but it is impossible to resist the temptation to give Fisher's presentation of the facts as he prepared it in submitting his case to the Royal Commission that afterwards investigated this deplorable miscarriage of a brilliant operation.

When Fisher sent me a summary of his evidence, I realised that, during all the anxious months of discussion of the project, he had been worried by the course that events were taking. He had failed, as events showed, to make his point of view clear to the Prime Minister and the War Cabinet. His concern was increased when he learned that special types of men-of-war ships which had been ingeniously designed for his great frontal attack on Germany by way of the Baltic were being jeopardised in the Dardanelles operations.

In this memorandum the First Sea Lord stated that he and the First Lord had worked in absolute accord at the Admiralty until it came to the question of the Dardanelles.

I was absolutely unable to give the Dardanelles proposal any welcome, for there was the Nelsonic dictum that "any sailor who attacked a fort was a fool."

My direct personal knowledge of the Dardanelles problem dates back many years. I had had the great advantage of commanding a battleship under Admiral Sir Geoffrey Phipps-Hornby when, during the Russo-Turkish War, that celebrated flag officer took the Fleet through the Dardanelles.

I had again knowledge of the subject as Commander-in-Chief of the Mediterranean Fleet for three years during the Boer War, when for a long period the Fleet under my command lay at Lemnos, off the mouth of the Dardanelles, thus affording me means of close study of the feasibility of forcing the Straits.

When I became First Sea Lord on October 20th, 1904, there arrived that very day the news of the Dogger Bank incident with Russia.

In my official capacity, in view of the possibility of a war with Russia, I immediately examined the question of the forcing of the Dardanelles, and I satisfied myself at that time that, even with military co-operation, the operation was mighty hazardous.

Basing myself on the experience gained over so many years, when the project was mooted in the present war my opinion was that the attempt to force the Dardanelles would not succeed.

I was the only member of the War Council who dissented from the project, but I did not carry my dissent to the point of resignation, because I understood that there were overwhelming political reasons why the attempt at least should be made.

Moreover, I felt it to be of vital importance that I should personally see to the completion of the great shipbuilding programme which was then under construction, which had been initiated by me on my advent to the Admiralty, and which included no less than 612 vessels.

The change in my opinion as to the relative importance of the probable failure in the Dardanelles began when the ever-increasing drain upon the Fleet, as the result of the prosecution of the Dardanelles undertaking, reached a point at which in my opinion it destroyed the possibility of the other naval operations which I had in view, and even approached to jeopardising our naval supremacy in the decisive theatre of the war.

I may be pressed with the question, Why did I not carry my objections to the point of resignation when the decision was first reached to attack the Dardanelles with naval force?

In my judgment it is not the business of the chief technical advisers of the Government to resign because their advice is not accepted, unless they are of opinion that the operation proposed must lead to disastrous results.

The attempt to force the Dardanelles, though a failure, would not have been disastrous so long as the ships employed could be withdrawn at any moment, and only such vessels were engaged, as in the beginning of the operations was in fact the case, as could be spared without detriment to the general service of the Fleet.

I may next be asked whether I made any protest at the War Council when the First Lord proposed the Dardanelles enterprise, or at any later date.

Mr. Churchill knew my opinion. I did not think it would tend towards good relations between the First Lord and myself, nor to the smooth working of the Board of Admiralty, to raise objections in the War Council's discussions. My opinion being known to Mr. Churchill in what I regarded as the proper constitutional way, I preferred thereafter to remain silent.

When the operation was undertaken, my duty from that time onwards was confined to seeing that the Government plan was carried out as successfully as possible with the available means.

I did everything I could to secure its success, and I only resigned when the drain it was making on the resources of the Navy became so great as to jeopardise the major operations of the Fleet.

On May 14th, 1915, the War Council made it clear to me that the great projects in Northern waters which I had in view in laying down the Armada of new vessels were at an end, and the further drain on our naval resources foreshadowed that evening convinced me that I could no longer countenance the Dardanelles operations, and the next day I resigned.

It seemed to me that I was faced at last by a progressive frustration of my main scheme of naval strategy.

Gradually the crowning work of war construction was being diverted and perverted from its original aim. The monitors, for instance, planned for the banks and shallows of Northern waters, were sent off to the Mediterranean, where they had never been meant to operate.

I felt I was right in remaining in office until this situation, never contemplated at first by anyone, was accepted by the War Council.   I felt right in resigning on this decision.

My conduct and the interpretation of my responsibility I respectfully submit to the judgment of the Committee. Perhaps I may be allowed to say that as regards the opinion I held, I was right.

The attack on the Dardanelles, conceived as an *amphibious operation of surprise* with the magnificent troops which were afterwards employed, should have succeeded and, in that event, the length of the war would undoubtedly have been shortened.   This incident, as I have said, led Fisher to resign, and then came the resignation of the First Lord.   I have recalled in an earlier page my visit to Mr. Churchill in his temporary home in Cromwell Road on the morning after his retirement became known.[1]   All that he had done for the Navy was seemingly forgotten by the nation.

Not the least serious aspect of the Dardanelles disaster, a brilliant strategic stroke of policy which miscarried, was that it robbed the country in an hour of supreme trial of two men of genius.   Fisher was so far advanced in years that his relinquishment of office at this juncture was merely the anticipation of an event which would have occurred in the course of nature in a short time.   But Churchill was in the prime of life.   He had served with distinction as a soldier with the Spaniards in Cuba in 1895, and as an officer of the British Army in India and Egypt and South Africa; he had acted as war correspondent of the *Morning Post*; filled with credit the position of Under-Secretary to the Colonies; been promoted to the office of President of the Board of Trade, thus entering the Cabinet as its youngest member; and he had acted as Home Secretary for a short and hectic period before becoming First Lord of the Admiralty.

Had his term at the Admiralty been a success, or a failure?   The impression of most people, knowing little of his record of achievement, was that he would not be greatly

[1] Page 49 *ante.*

missed; he was troublesome and impatient of the wisdom of older and more experienced men. But he had left his mark on the whole war effort. He had shown imagination and driving power. He had had the courage to fight in the Cabinet the Chancellor of the Exchequer, Lloyd George, for Navy Estimates which were unparalleled in their commitments. He had been responsible for shipbuilding programmes which turned the scale against the Germans in the later phase of the struggle. He foresaw the rôle which the aeroplane would play in warfare, and when the War Office looked askance on the idea of the tank, he had appointed a committee under Sir Eustace Tennyson D'Eyncourt, the Director of Naval Construction, to consider designs. He had also given the Navy its own oil supplies.

He was criticised at the time for interfering with the experts in every office that he held. It may have been true, but, if so, it was because he had qualities which they did not possess. He could not sit content while men of mediocre calibre dilly-dallied. To his critics at this period he might have replied, "How would the country have fared if it had not had the Naval Staff, the Naval Air Service, the Anglo-Persian Oil supplies and the tank, for all of which I was responsible?"

In later years he was Minister of Munitions, successively Secretary of State for War, the Air and the Colonies, and then, having acted as Chancellor of the Exchequer from 1924 to 1929, in the Baldwin Government, it seemed to many people that his political career had come to an end. He had left the Liberals, to the chagrin of the party. He had apparently come to the conclusion that with the rise of the Socialists it had no future; the country would tolerate only two parties. At that time, still a Free Trader, he was distrusted by his new friends among the Conservatives. He was the Ishmail of the political world. He retained his seat in the House of Commons, however, and when he spoke the benches filled, since he was the outstanding Parliamentary orator of the time. But he had apparently no

following in Parliament or in the country. The electors
of the Epping Division of Essex, for which he had sat since
1924, remained faithful (the voters of Dundee having
rejected him two years earlier). But for the rest, he was
friendless.

During the years when he was banished from the Councils
of the State, he devoted himself to writing a succession of
brilliant volumes—"The World Crisis" and "Marlborough"
pre-eminent among them. Never before had any historian
been courted so persistently by publishers on both sides of
the Atlantic, or paid such large royalties. Thus, with characteristic industry, he devoted his abilities to the making of
books, throwing off an occasional newspaper article and
finding recreation in painting and bricklaying.

Who foresaw that this soldier, author, orator and states-
man, with great qualities of head and heart, was in the
hour of his country's ordeal to be called to the office of
Prime Minister in 1940 by the voice of a united nation?
He had fought, first with the Conservatives, then with the
Liberals, and had at last returned to the Conservative fold.
A turncoat! The British people do not like turncoats.
Yet this man of destiny was chosen by acclamation as leader
of the Conservative Party after he had been accepted by
the Socialists as the head of a Coalition Administration.

His return to office as Prime Minister was the most
dramatic incident in British political history. The statesman who had had no friends attained in a few months, by
his magnetic personality, a position of respect and authority
in the hearts of the peoples of the Empire which no former
Prime Minister of any democracy had ever reached. It was
realised that, for the first time, the British Empire had a
leader who had presided over every important department
in the State, and possessed an unrivalled knowledge of war
by sea, land and air. In the formation of his Government,
he exhibited uncanny powers; though the Conservatives
were in overwhelming majority in the House of Commons
and entrenched in the House of Lords, the Socialists were

given four of the key positions in his Administration, and thus the whole-hearted co-operation of the workers was ensured. It became a people's war.

Winston Spencer Churchill, the despair of party hench-men, appeared before the world as the idol of his country. Even Pitt in his zenith of power in the Napoleonic Wars never reached such a position of unchallenged supremacy in the affairs of the State. After wandering in many byways in the world of politics, he had reached the path his father, Lord Randolph Churchill, a statesman in advance of his time, had trodden. He had become the outstanding Conservative democrat, the statesman of progress by evolu-tion, interpreting the ideals of the sanest men of all parties and differing only from the Socialists in methods.

Winston Churchill's disappearance from public life in 1915 was to be only temporary, but the resignation of Fisher meant the end of his career in the service of the nation.

The Board of Admiralty was reconstituted, Balfour becoming First Lord in place of Churchill. The Fisher régime in naval affairs, which had had such far-reaching results, came to an end. He had threatened to resign once too often, and he had resigned at a moment when he should not have done so or in the way that he did. And I think that he himself regretted afterwards that he had not dealt with the situation in a more diplomatic manner; for he never ceased to desire to be in harness again, in spite of his advanced age.

He was pleased with little that happened in subsequent years. He was disappointed by the Battle of Jutland, he disapproved of Jellicoe relinquishing the command of the Grand Fleet in order to become First Sea Lord, and he entertained to the end confidence that he could have done better at the Admiralty than his successors in the position of First Sea Lord. It may be that he was right, for he had a flair for doing the right thing at the right moment and in the right way, but the opportunity never came. He never believed that he had been defeated by age or anything else. He watched closely, occasionally putting his spoke in the official wheel, sometimes in what seemed a spirit of mischief.

When he was staying with the Duke and Duchess of Hamilton at Balcombe Place, I sent him something I had written. In reply I received this letter, written, as usual, in his own hand and not typed.

BALCOMBE PLACE,
BALCOMBE,
SUSSEX.

MY DEAR HURD,

　　　Your article is delicious, but no one reads articles nowadays. Criticism is at an end—Parliament is gagged— the Press is frightened—the Public apathetic—as the Germans have not yet ravished their women and life in England is as usual!

I have the credit of sending Asquith to bed with 4 letters I wrote. Balfour got them suppressed for a while, and so the effect "fizzled out" as regards the immediate effect, but they will be d—d unpleasant some day. I wish you could read them. Lloyd George says he has never read anything like them! But what good? There is no "push"! Passivity, as Winston said, is the Admiralty motto, and the Germans are sinking ships freely. I am vegetating here. I find it maddening being in London—powerless and cast out—and yet never in such vigour in all my life! And such a new complexion could be given to the war!

The "God-sent" fall of Tirpitz at one hour's notice is another proof we are the Lost Ten Tribes of Israel. The German Fleet would have been out this week with the new moon and all England frightened by half a million of German soldiers in the Hamburg transports—and Jellicoe can't stir a yard without being spotted by the new Zeppelins, whose radius of action goes far beyond Scapa Flow with bombs that wouldn't leave much of Jellicoe if dropped on the *Iron Duke.*

Jan. 7, 1915. I resigned on this Zeppelin menace and put in a paper predicting the present situation to the War Council. But I was forced to remain. I also foretold the *Goeben* 4 years ago on April 22, 1912! A lovely letter!

Fisher
Admiral of the Fleet
Dec. 8. 1914

Being the Anniversary of the Annihilation of Admiral Von Spee's Squadron whereby Nitrates came to England to make our Munitions & be produced — Africa was Saved — and a Second Coaling avoided at the Falkland Islands and our Commerce Saved in all the Southern Oceans! The "Dreadnought" Battle Cruisers that sunk Admiral Von Spee had not a man killed or wounded! Yet I do not turn and rend my Detractors — I leave them one and all to the Worm that gnaweth!

INSCRIPTION BY LORD FISHER IN A PRESENTATION COPY OF HIS BOOK "RECORDS"

Jellicoe
AF

Colonel House suggested my going to America. I think
I may.

Yours always,
FISHER.
29.3.16.

You'd better bring your wife and daughter here to
lunch—the Duke will be so delighted and will send to meet
you at Balcombe Station or Haywards Heath. (Not to-
morrow Thursday, as I shall be away.)

In the following year (May 20th, 1917) I had another
letter from him which showed that he was watching and
waiting and hoping, as I believe, for a recall to the
Admiralty.

DEAR HURD,

. . . Nemesis is on the heels of Jellicoe for allowing
himself to be cajoled by Balfour to leave the Grand Fleet
where he was incomparable and for which for 13 years I
had pestered every First Lord to fit him for and with
success! Alas! Alas! I sometimes feel when I think these
things over like Elijah when he went that day's journey
into the wilderness and sat under the Juniper Tree and
requested for himself that he might die! and you'll
remember "an angel touched him and said, Arise and eat"
—that meant that he was to "*keep fit*"! and his day would
come and it did! So I solace myself with these words (but
I don't want to go to Heaven just yet as Elijah did! *He
was a Great man, Elijah!*). I always like the way he shut
up Elisha and told him to mind his own business. Well.
The German air-craft are over Folkestone and as they get
daily more powerful engines they'll go further and carry
bigger bombs! *Shall we never learn?*
Had the Admiralty proposal in *November 1914* been
carried out (it was approved but smashed by the Dardanelles
adventure)—of the British Army advancing along the sea-
shore flanked by the British Fleet, there would never have
been a submarine menace nor these air-raids and we should
have recaptured Antwerp. Sir John French was had over
3 times to the War Council and concurred to carry it out,
asking only for 2 Divisions, but again I was foiled! *It*

11

will have to be done now! No "dug outs" for the Germans there, like at the Somme, for when you go down a few feet you come to water, so our Artillery ashore and afloat dominate the situation. They ask me for my Plan. I reply in the immortal words of Mr. Burke:

> "I have no faith in any scheme of war in which the 'Execution' is divorced from the Plan."

or better still, as my friend Sir Bertrand Dawson says to me:

> "Don't prescribe till you're called in!"

He came to say goodbye to me the other day before going over to France, and kindly assured me I was fitter in mind and body than when he examined me 10 years ago! "And of such is the Kingdom of Heaven!" As we are made worse of on earth!

Yours,
FISHER.
20.5.17.

P.S.—Hankey tells me he recently found a letter of mine written in *1910* saying that Asquith would be turned out in *November 1916*!

His mind and his time, fortunately, were occupied by his work as chairman of the Board of Invention and Research, to which he had been appointed—a task for which he was, in spite of his age, pre-eminently suited. I have preserved one letter written on August 31st, 1918, because in it he revealed himself as young in all but years, and still looking into the future and planning for it.

MY DEAR HURD,
       Excuse the writing paper—I am out of doors—with the moor all round me, wishing I was never going to leave such an Elysium! but this d—d Board of Research takes me back to London (3, Eaton Square) to-morrow Wednesday. I won't deny there are some very big things that this Board may bring forth—McKenna firmly believes we shall devise some wonderful scheme by which on a button being pressed the whole fabric of the German Empire crumbles into

dust!   And then he says to me, "You are still the idol of the Nation, and you will be recalled by acclamation to the hearts of the people."   (Perhaps you did not know that the Chancellor of the Exchequer hid this poetic strain in his nature!)

Both Balfour and Asquith have been and were most cordial, but the Dardanelles is the skeleton in the cupboard which haunts them.   I am the skeleton!   So there is no communion of hearts at present.

I cannot understand how the whole British Press, fully acquainted with the disastrous consequences attendant upon such a criminal adventure, has gone on backing up the butchery now in progress with absolutely no commensurate result, however successful—on the contrary, we give Constantinople to a huge Power like Russia instead of to Bulgaria.   However, no use expatiating on this further. Bonar Law has had Winston Churchill to spend the week-end with him!

"And the same Pilate and Herod were made friends together: for before they were at enmity between themselves."—St. Luke, Chap. 23, Verse 12.

In the following year, while he was again in Sussex, Fisher wrote to me another characteristic communication on affairs:

Never did any man hate another as Bonar Law hated Winston, and his condition of the Coalition was that Winston should not be in the Cabinet and a friend of your First Lord in his place; however, Balfour stood out for Winston because of the Dardanelles.   (You had better burn this.)

Your kind letter and its enclosure most acceptable.   I don't want to be egotistical, but there is the stubborn fact that the 6 years from 1904 to 1910 gave us the Navy that has now swept the seas, and without undue arrogance I can say—

"Alone I did it."

I put my faith in the 51st Chap. of Jeremiah, "The Lord God of Recompences shall surely requite."

Though I'm afraid we've got to wait for the day of

Judgment! Even now to-day a Big Policy would end the War! But there is no Big Mind!

In a letter at the beginning of 1920, I sent him my good wishes for the New Year, and I recalled briefly all that he had done. The war was over, won by the power exercised by the British Navy, and he could feel that he was "on the crest of the wave." He replied:

As you say, to be on the crest of the wave at the latter end is interesting. I got an immense ovation at "Pinafore," and some passing man said to my friend, "My, how popular he is," illustrating Jeremiah's saying—"It is good for a man to bear the yoke in his youth!" (Lamentations 3. 24).

When on July 13th of that year I heard the "Last Post" blown by a bugler in the recesses of Westminster Abbey as the great sailor and naval administrator was laid to rest, I knew that the most stirring and dramatic chapter in my life had closed. The final hymn which was sung during the service was appropriate to the man:

> Now the labourer's task is o'er,
> Now the battle-day is past;
> Now upon the further shore
> Lands the voyager at last.
> Father, in Thy gracious keeping
> Leave we now Thy servant sleeping.

Owing to Fisher's life's devotion to his country, we continued to sleep quietly in our beds until, under Hitler, the Germans made another attempt to dominate Europe. But in the war that opened on September 3rd, 1939, the enemy possessed no such fleet as had been mobilised on August 3rd, 1914. The task of the Royal Navy, though it fought in lonely isolation, without a friend, was more simple so far as the major issue was concerned, for it was certain that there would be no fleet action. On the other hand, it was complicated and rendered more difficult by the greater perfection of the U-boat for purposes of piracy, and by the development of the bombing aeroplane, and the use by the enemy of more deadly mines, some of them dropped from the air.

CHAPTER IX

SHIPS AND MANY OTHER THINGS

In the year preceding the outbreak of the war of 1914–18 Mr. (afterwards Sir) Westcott Abell [1] moved from Liverpool University, where he was Professor of Naval Architecture, to London. His new post was that of Chief Ship Surveyor of Lloyd's Register, the oldest of all the organisations for the classification of shipping. He became a near neighbour of mine at Hampstead, and began my education in shipping matters, to which I had hitherto given little thought. I could not have had a better instructor, for among the younger men of his profession he stood out as of conspicuous ability. He was trained at the Royal Engineering College at Devonport, he had served for several years in the Royal Corps of Naval Constructors, acting for a time as assistant to Sir Philip Watts when Director of Naval Construction, and later had been lecturer on the design and building of men-of-war at the Royal Naval College at Greenwich from 1907 to 1910.

It is unnecessary to trace the evolution of Lloyd's Register as a co-operative and protective institution from the days when those interested in merchant shipping used to meet in Lloyd's Coffee House. It represents underwriters, shipowners and shipbuilders; through its committees it ensures that ships are so designed that they will withstand the hazards of the sea. With its national committees in the United States and other countries and its surveyors in every port of importance throughout the world, it has become in course of time a great international organisation for promoting safety at sea. Within a stone's throw of its head-

---

[1] Received the K.B.E. in 1920 for his services during the war of 1914-18.

quarters is the Baltic Exchange, the centre at which most of the chartering of tonnage of the tramp type is arranged.

As Chief Ship Surveyor of Lloyd's Register, Abell occupied, therefore, a position of great responsibility. Its importance was increased by the outbreak of the war in 1914. Owing to the intensive U-boat campaign of the Germans, the issue of the struggle resolved itself at last into a race to build ships in this country sufficiently quickly to replace the losses as they were sustained at sea. On that victory or defeat, in the final issue, depended.

I had always shared the widespread feeling that ship-owners were well able to look after themselves, and that, in doing so, they had not always shown much consideration for their officers, for their men or for the nation. Under the old Navigation Acts they had been protected against competition in trading between the British Isles and overseas parts of the Empire, and the industry had, in consequence, suffered. In the early years of the nineteenth century, the condition of the Merchant Navy was a national peril. As a result of enquiries in the principal ports of the world, which were instituted in 1843 by Mr. James Murray, an official of the Foreign Office, a deplorable state of affairs was revealed. Mr. Murray summed up the results of his investigations in these words:

It is stated from various parts of the world that persons placed in command of British ships are so habitually addicted to drunkenness as to be unfitted for their position, and it will be seen that Her Majesty's Consuls allude specifically to the notorious and gross intemperance, and to the ignorance and brutality of British ship-masters, many of whom are totally void of education. In several reports it is stated that there are honourable exceptions to the unworthy class of masters, thus showing that among British masters frequenting foreign ports bad conduct and ignorance is the rule, and intelligence and ability the exception; that, on the other hand, foreign masters are educated, sober, intelligent men, capable of commanding their ships, and that foreign seamen are consequently more orderly.

Mr. Samuel Plimsoll carried on the movement for reform, protesting against what he described as "coffin ships," which put to sea in such an unseaworthy state that they were never heard of again. Later Mr. Joseph Chamberlain, as President of the Board of Trade, submitted to the House of Commons a bill to provide "greater security of life and property at sea." He told a story which shocked the nation. A minority of shipowners—for he made it clear that it was only a minority—had taken every advantage of the ineffective laws which, in the words of a lawyer of the time, declared in effect to the shipowner with an easy conscience, "buy your ship as cheaply as you can, equip her as poorly as you can, load her as fully as you can and send her to sea. If she gets to the end of her voyage, you will make a very good thing of it; if she goes to the bottom, you will have made a much better thing of it."

The ill repute which such men had brought on the industry as a whole persisted down to the eve of the war of 1914–18. Shipowners were regarded askance by many people as though they were all black sheep, whereas by that time, even if there was still room for improvement in the pay and the conditions of life of officers and men, the industry was being conducted in an honourable manner. Shipowners had arisen who abominated the way in which so many ships had once been sent to sea. They co-operated whole-heartedly with underwriters and shipbuilders through Lloyd's Register, and in every other feasible way to wipe out the reproach of the past. Under their enlightened management the industry prospered and expanded.

When Abell took up his appointment at Lloyd's Register, nearly one-half of the steam tonnage of the world was owned in this country. That position had been attained without subsidy or any form of protection, in competition with the other merchant marines of the world. It was the reward of a high standard of efficiency in construction, manning and operating. In shipbuilding this country's position was even more notable, since in the preceding twenty years two-thirds of all the ships afloat had been launched from the yards of the United Kingdom. Shipowners and shipbuilders worked in conditions of complete freedom from Government control, except in so far as safety regulations were concerned, and the last thing of which they had a thought was that in war-time they might be put into the strait-waistcoat of bureaucracy.

In the early months of the struggle shipowners continued to carry on much as usual, under the spur of the acquisitive instinct, which is the basis of success in any business. The industry served the nation efficiently; the fullest use was made of the tonnage available after the needs of the Admiralty and War Office for auxiliaries and transports had been met. Owners in this as well as other countries made large profits. As ships were sunk by the enemy and the supply of tonnage, British, Allied and neutral, decreased, the law of supply and demand raised freights. It was an inevitable movement from which shipowners in all Allied and neutral countries benefited.

Sir Arthur Salter, M.P., who was not conspicuously friendly to shipowners, admitted in his monograph on "Allied Shipping Control," "No blame whatever can attach to shipowners for taking the rates which were current at this period of the war." Until the Government became the purchaser of essential supplies, shipowners, like other people whose trade was favourably affected by the war, took what the gods gave them by way of freight. They were engaged in ordinary trading with such tonnage as the Government did not require, and received no more than the world rates; if some philanthropists had taken less, they would merely have been putting more money into the pockets of the merchants who bought and sold the goods. The consumer, even to the limited extent to which the cost of sea carriage added to the retail price of what he purchased, would have been no better off. Many owners favoured a scheme for limitation of freights, because they realised that the situation was one that was liable to create public prejudice owing to failure of the average man and woman to realise, first, that the shipowner was merely the "victim of circumstances," and, secondly, that his profits distributed over the whole of the cargoes which he carried had little effect on prices in the shops.

During the early period of the Great War, Mr. Walter Runciman [1] was President of the Board of Trade, and therefore was responsible for merchant shipping. I met him first when my friend Gerald France, M.P., was his Parliamentary Secretary. I was struck by his cold manner as well as by the insight with which he dealt with any subject, no matter what it was; but as I came to know him better I realised that he was a friend whose regard would stand the test of circumstances. That his abilities won the respect of successive Prime Ministers is apparent from his career as a servant of the nation, for he was almost continuously in office from 1905 until the beginning of 1940. His services to the State, which nearly cost him his life, may never be realised, for only those who knew him well appreciated his goodness of heart, his intellect and his sound judgment, on which one Prime Minister after another relied.

In that early part of the war the Government relations with merchant shipping were regulated by the Marine Department, of which Sir Charles Hipwood had charge. He possessed in a remarkable degree the judicial mind. He was always accessible to shipowners, and when occasion arose, to shipbuilders; he would hear all they had to say with patience as the umpire representing the taxpayers, travellers by sea, and merchants who employ ships for the carriage of their goods, as well as underwriters. These were months of ordeal for the Marine Department, for the course of events at sea, with the appearance of the U-boat, could not have been foreseen and provided for. The country had at its disposal what was believed to be an ample volume of tonnage. In the circumstances, the wise

[1] Created Viscount Runciman of Doxford 1940.

course was to leave the industry to carry on as it had done
in previous wars, thus gaining the full benefits of the
knowledge and experience of the managers and their staffs
as well as of their respective organisations, and especially of
the "clubs," which existed for the purpose of mutual aid.

For twenty-six months the shipping industry continued
to compete in the world's markets, and made large profits.
Runciman could have intervened, but he had been brought
up in the industry, and knew that interference might limit
the earnings and lead to a loss of efficiency. So shipping as
well as shipbuilding remained free. It was the success of
the U-boats that brought about Government control, and
the resultant loss in carrying capacity. When the Government
became the buyer of practically all essential supplies for the
fighting forces as well as the civil population, the control by
the State of the shipping industry was an inevitable development, and shipbuilding had also to be regulated as a matter
of course.

On Lloyd George becoming Prime Minister in 1917,
he decided that nothing mattered but victory, and that
victory must be gained as soon as possible—before our
strength was exhausted. So the shipping industry passed
under the Government without any regard to its economic
future. It was a new experience. During former wars, the
nation had gone on living much as usual. The Napoleonic
Wars were for us predominantly maritime, and so were
the two China Wars, the Crimean War, the Indian Mutiny,
the Abyssinian Campaign, the Ashanti War, the Zulu War,
the first Boer War, the Egyptian Campaigns, and the war
in South Africa of 1899–1902. The troops employed were
supplied by the small Regular Army, and were carried in
transports which were hired by the Government at commercial rates.

The Great War which opened in 1914 was the first total
war in which we had taken part, engaging all our resources,
and especially the shipping industry; it submerged for the
time all economic considerations. The normal activities of

one industry after another were diverted to the one purpose, and thus it came about that shipping was caught in the stream and the Government took charge of it, liners as well as tramps. That meant the setting up of a new department —the Ministry of Shipping, which was housed in temporary buildings in the Green Park, an ugly range of bungalows.

The extent to which the shipping industry was affected by this change in our practice has never been fully realised. It was a radical departure from a purely maritime policy. A large Expeditionary Force was sent across the English Channel in the hope of saving France from being overrun by the German Army. That decision and our obligations to our Allies meant the absorption of a great volume of shipping.

How deeply British shipping, in July 1918, was pledged to the service of the Allies will appear from a comparison of the proportions in which the various Powers contributed to, and drew from, the tonnage pool. The total steam shipping under the British, French and Italian flags on July 31st amounted, exclusive of ships repairing or un-employed, to about 21,600,000 tons deadweight, of which 27 per cent. was on naval or military service, and 13 per cent. was employed in the coasting or colonial trade or in the import service of other Allies, the United States or neutrals. In view of the increased American trooping programme, no reduction could be expected in the pro-portion on naval and military services, and the colonial trades had already been drastically combed, both by the French and British authorities.

There remained available for employment in the import services of the three countries just under 13,000,000 tons deadweight; but to this must be added 2,500,000 tons of shipping under other flags. The total tonnage available for fulfilment of the import programme was thus 15,500,000 tons. Of this, 72 per cent. was British, 11 per cent. was French or Italian, and the remainder was about equally divided between neutral tonnage and tonnage contributed by the United States or by other Allies, such as Japan, Belgium, Portugal or Brazil.

Very different were the proportions in which the tonnage was allocated. Of the whole 15,500,000 tons, only 57 per cent. was in the import service of the United Kingdom, who contributed nearly three-quarters of the pool; 43 per cent. was in the service of France and Italy, who contributed less than one-eighth. Although 27 per cent. of British tonnage was on naval or military service, very little of the shipping provided by the United States and the minor Allies or procured from neutrals was claimed by Great Britain, and no less than 92 per cent. of the tonnage in the import service of the United Kingdom was under the British flag. On the other hand, British shipping provided 47 per cent. of the tonnage in French and Italian service, or nearly twice as much as was provided by French and Italian shipping.[1]

This statement of the position at sea emphasises one dominant fact. But for the extent to which British investors had provided tonnage in the years before the outbreak of the war, often in periods of depression receiving no dividends, neither this country nor its Allies could have continued the struggle in face of Germany's intensive submarine campaign. The U-boats, in association with mines and raiders, destroyed British, Allied and neutral vessels of nearly 13,000,000 tons. For the first time in our history, in spite of our dependence on overseas supplies being greater than that of any other country, a large portion of tonnage had to be used by the armies sent overseas or lent to the Allies. The peoples of the British Empire, much less the governments of France and Italy, have never adequately appreciated their debt to the British shipping industry.

It was when these conditions were developing, that at length the Government took over control of all seagoing ships. How could so exceptional an industry, with ramifications in every sea and ocean of the world, and a peculiar technique, be mobilised for war with the least loss of efficiency, even though its economic foundations were undermined? One of the wisest decisions of Lloyd George was to

[1] "Seaborne Trade" (Official History), by C. Ernest Fayle.

put a shipowner at the head of the new department. There were many shipowners whose names were household words. The Prime Minister's choice fell on a Scotsman who had taken little or no part in political affairs, and was unknown outside shipping circles. He was not a great figure even in that little world; he had been occupied mainly in managing a modest fleet of tramp ships and in philanthropy on a generous scale. It was a matter of surprise, therefore, when it was announced that Sir Joseph Maclay was coming from Glasgow to London as the new Minister of Shipping.

Afterwards it became known that he had only accepted the office on his own terms. He would not go into the House of Commons to represent his Ministry; he would not agree to sit in the House of Lords; he would not consent to be subject to the authority of any other department. He laid it down as an essential condition that he should be free to shape his own policy in sympathy with the general policy of the Government, and should have direct access to the Prime Minister. On these conditions, hitherto undreamed of in the bureaucratic world, Maclay began the organisation of his department. With sound judgment he gathered round him many of the leaders of the shipping world, so as to enlist their whole-hearted support and the co-operation of their staffs. In this way, with the willing aid of a group of Civil Servants, he hoped to preserve an essential national industry from the worst effects of Government control.

The Civil Servants of this country are supreme in their own sphere. What is sometimes called "red tape" is an essential feature of administration, when every action may be subject to subsequent enquiry by Parliament and every item of expenditure may be submitted to close examination by the Auditor-General and possibly by a Select Committee of the House of Commons. The Civil Servant is bound to walk warily and to walk slowly. He is governed by rules and regulations which are necessary, however irritating they may appear to the business man who is answerable only to himself and his partners, and possibly once a year to such shareholders as may attend the annual meeting of the company over which he presides. The very virtues of the Civil Service, its meticulous care over details and its deliberate methods, are its defects in the commercial sphere, in which initiative and quick decisions, based on knowledge of markets, are the secrets of success.

How Maclay came to realise that, if he was to succeed as Minister of Shipping, he must keep the Civil Servant in his place as administrator is a secret, for he had had no previous knowledge of Government departments. It may have been the intuition of the Scot. At any rate, he organised his department in sections, each of which was under a shipowner with knowledge and experience. On one and all he impressed the fact that they were for the time being the servants, even if the unpaid servants, of the State in the trial of strength which was going on at sea. The manner in which they worked in unfamiliar harness assured the success of the administration.

The Minister of Shipping was not a man of whom success would have been prophesied. He was a lifelong teetotaller, he did not smoke, he was in no sense a man of the world. He had deep religious convictions, and was unswerving in his loyalty to his principles. Maclay's abstinence from alcoholic liquor and from the soothing influence of nicotine made it all the more surprising that, in his position of absolute authority, he drew to himself men of such varied character. It was no doubt his transparent goodness.

He bore some resemblance to Walter Runciman, who was also a teetotaller and a Nonconformist. After the war, a speaker at a dinner at which they were both present complimented them on the contributions which they had made to victory. Their success had surprised him. A man who takes a glass of beer with his meals, the speaker continued, leans back when he has finished eating and drinking, feeling a gentle glow over his body. "This is a good world," he thinks, and takes his ease knowing that the food he has eaten will be digested without trouble. But the man who has drunk only water rises with the conviction that his stomach, unassisted by alcohol, has a lot of work to do and may give him awkward sensations. "This is a rotten world," he declares to himself. "I will see if I can't do something to set it right." And thus, said the speaker, revolutions begin. He suggested that since the President of the Board of Trade and the Minister of Shipping had got on so well with their colleagues and the staffs in their departments, and had started no rebellions in or out of the Governments of which they were members, all the more credit was due to them because they had had no alcohol to soothe them.

When the Ministry was near its end after the war, what was described as "a farewell dinner" to the Minister was held. I have attended many dinners, but this was unique in the tribute which was offered to this man of simple tastes, but by no means simple mind. He had won everyone's heart, from the most dominating shipowner, an individualist to his finger-tips, objecting to any interference, to the leaders of the merchant officers' organisations and of the seamen's trade union. They were all represented at that dinner, which we believed signalised the winding up of this extemporised department. But we were quite wrong. The Ministry continued in existence for some time. Maclay knew that there was a powerful movement for the nationalisation of shipping. It was supported by influential members of the Cabinet. The Admiralty also nursed the hope that it might be placed in charge of merchant shipping when nationalised. Maclay was determined to remain at the helm until this movement had been defeated. So, though the farewell dinner had been held, he continued to be Minister of Shipping until all possibility of nationalisation was at an end. It was only then that he resigned.

As shipowners who had supported the Minister drifted back to their offices, they realised that, though the Ministry had been the most successful of all the new departments, the war had left to them troubles such as had never confronted them before. The eclipse of British sea power in its commercial aspect had begun while they had been busy in the bungalows in the Green Park, and they were confronted with the problem of re-establishing their services in all parts of the world in face of competition much more intense than they had experienced in the past.

Shipbuilders were less fortunate than shipowners. As soon as the U-boat crisis developed in the spring of 1917, Mr. Lloyd George placed all the shipyards under the Admiralty, though work was making good progress under Sir Joseph Maclay, with a staff of about thirty officials who were experts and worked amicably with the Marine Department of the Board of Trade, Lloyd's Register of Shipping and kindred organisations. The Prime Minister wanted a hustle, and he got it. Sir Eric Geddes, who knew nothing of the industry—a very technical industry—was appointed Controller of Shipbuilding and Repairs, both naval and commercial, and he was soon in command of an enormous staff. Major-General C. S. Collard, R.E., was made Deputy Controller of Auxiliary Shipbuilding, including mercantile construction, though he also had had no experience in a shipyard or engine shop.

Plans were made for building ships of concrete. A scheme was drawn up for national shipyards at Chepstow, Beachley and Portbury, where forty-one vessels, termed "fabricated ships," could be building simultaneously by German prisoners, working under more or less expert supervision. There was wild talk of an aggregate output in the old and new yards of 3,000,000 tons in a year. But progress depended not on hustlers, but on skilled workers and steel. So, though the cost of all these measures was high and the Prime Minister was gratified by the appearance of something being done, the main result of these expedients was that the industry was thrown on its beam ends. The men who did know how to build ships resented the suggestion that theirs was an easy task, especially as they were required to surrender workmen and steel which they could have used to better advantage for the Government's "hustle." All they desired was to go on building ships as quickly as possible. They had to manage as best they could amid the confusion of projects. The output in the year was only 1,163,000 tons, about the figure which Sir Joseph Maclay had considered possible.

About this time I had a talk with the Prime Minister at 10, Downing Street. Mr. Lloyd George was in an irritable frame of mind, and uttered the threat that he would nationalise the shipbuilding industry if the leaders did not toe the line. But, at last, he evidently realised that he had made a mistake. And he took the course which should have been adopted at first. He sought the assistance of a shipbuilder—Lord Pirrie, the outstanding figure in the industry, who had risen from apprentice to be head of the great firm of Harland & Wolff, at Belfast. He became Controller-General of Merchant Shipbuilding, with a seat on the Board of Admiralty and direct access, like Sir Joseph Maclay, to the Cabinet.

Lord Pirrie, with a twinkle in his eye, afterwards told me a story which illustrated Eric Geddes's method of dealing with any difficulty. His plan was always to increase the staff. If I remember rightly, during his term as First Lord he doubled the staff at the Admiralty which his predecessor Carson had found adequate. However that may be, when Pirrie agreed to become Controller of Merchant Ship-building after so many errors of policy had been committed, he moved into a room at the Admiralty. Geddes was the Minister responsible for the department over which he was to preside. So the First Lord came in due course to see the new Controller.

"Now, Lord Pirrie, I hope you will tell me what you want in the matter of staff, because you must be well served." "Thank you, Sir Eric," Pirrie replied, in the soft Irish brogue which he never lost, "it is very good of you,

12

and I will let you know in the course of a few days—after
I have had an opportunity of seeing what staff there is."
A few days later the First Lord came again. "Well, Lord
Pirrie, have you decided what additions you would like to
make to your staff?" "You are very kind, Sir Eric," the
Controller replied. "I wonder if I might bring with me
to the Admiralty Miss ——, who has been my secretary
for several years and is a great help to me." "Oh yes,
certainly, but what other new people would you like," the
First Lord added. "Oh, that will be quite sufficient; with
Miss —— and the present staff I am sure I shall get along
nicely."

On seeing Lord Pirrie for the last time, when the war
was becoming a memory, I appreciated what an admirable
secretary he had. I was too early for my appointment at
the offices of the White Star Line in Cockspur Street, which
were his headquarters in London. At last Lord Pirrie
hurried into the waiting-room, full of apologies which were
not really due to me. He took my arm in his characteristic way, and we entered his room. We sat down on either
side of a table on which, in anticipation of the talk which
he had suggested that morning on the telephone, his
secretary had placed a dossier, with my name on it; it contained memoranda on all the subjects which he intended
to discuss, which included the possibilities of the Diesel
engine in merchant ships. Incidentally I may add that he
was the best salesman of ships—ships to be built—that
this country ever had at its service. In promoting the
interest of Harland & Wolff, he was promoting an important
branch of the export trade, employing a large number of
skilled craftsmen.

Under this leader the *tempo* of work in the shipyards
increased, and in 1918 the output was raised to 1,600,000
tons. The national shipyards, on which £2,800,000,000 had
been squandered, made no contribution to the total, and
concrete ships were exposed as a fraud, extravagantly costly.
When the war closed, Lord Pirrie had in hand a great

programme of construction which was moving methodically towards completion, and if the submarine had not been mastered and the armistice had not been signed, the nation would have had a deeper appreciation of what it owed to this charming and talented Ulsterman.

We pulled through the ordeal arising from the enemy's attack on shipping by the skin of our teeth. How much the nation owed to the seamen and the shipowners and shipbuilders, some of whom never recovered from the strain of these years, I did not realise until I came to write the official history of the part which the Merchant Navy had taken in the struggle, three big volumes of 1,337 pages, which have had probably fewer readers than any other book of its size published for many years. I accepted this task at the invitation of the Admiralty and the Board of Trade. The work it entailed nearly cost me my life. I had no idea of what was before me. I was frightened when I was first shown the room at the Board of Trade which was filled with files containing the record of each ship which had escaped after attack, had been damaged, or had been sunk. And, in addition to these dockets, there were the files at the Admiralty and the statements of merchant officers on landing which had, with great industry and meticulous care, been taken down by Mr. Martin Hill, of the Liverpool Steam Ship Owners' Association.

Apart from ships which escaped owing to the manner in which they were handled in face of the enemy, 2,479 vessels were sunk, and each one had its own story in the Board of Trade records, while in many instances reference had to be made to the Admiralty papers or to Mr. Martin Hill's narrative. Before the last volume was published, King George V had decided to create the position of Master of Merchant Shipping and the Fishing Fleets, to which the Prince of Wales was appointed. So a foreword by His Royal Highness seemed appropriate, in which he recorded his admiration of the seamen who, in ships not built for the violence of war, had refused at the point of death to surrender in face of unprecedented ruthlessness on the part of the enemy.

While Sir Joseph Maclay was Minister of Shipping, he usually lunched with some of his colleagues at the Royal Societies' Club, which was conveniently situated in St. James's Street. The committee welcomed them and, indeed, placed a sitting-room at their service, where they could talk for half an hour or so before returning to their desks. I well remember some of these interludes in the day's work. The conversation was by no means confined to shipping, but ranged over a wide field, and the Minister always took a shrewd part in it. Towards the end of the war it became the habit of some of us to meet at this club in the evening. When the Ministry was being wound up, Abell suggested that it was a pity that the links of friendship which had been cemented in preceding months should be severed. Could we not meet occasionally at dinner? Thus I became what would be described as compère of the XXI Dining Circle—so called because it was started in 1921 and had twenty-one members. Its original members were:

Sir Westcott Abell, Chief Ship Surveyor of Lloyd's Register of Shipping.

Sir Alan Anderson, Chairman of the Orient Steamship Company, afterwards M.P. for the City of London and Director of the Bank of England and of the Suez Canal Company.

Sydney Boulton, Chairman of Lloyd's.

Admiral Sir Douglas Brownrigg, Bt., Chief Naval Censor and, later, director of the Fairfield Shipbuilding and Engineering Company.

H. M. Cleminson, General Manager of the Chamber of Shipping.

Sir Gerald Chadwyck-Healey, Bt.

W. H. Dugdale.

Sir Andrew Duncan, Vice-President of the Shipbuilding Employers' Federation; President of the Board of Trade, 1939.

Commander Sir Thomas Fisher, London manager of Canadian Steamships (C.P.R.).

Gerald France, M.P.

Sir Ernest Glover, Bt., President of the Chamber of Shipping, 1923.

Lionel Hichens, Chairman of Cammell Laird & Co., large shipbuilders.

C. Hipwood, C.B., Secretary of the Marine Department of the Board of Trade; knighted in 1926.

Archibald Hurd; knighted in 1928.

Percy Hurd, M.P.; knighted in 1930.

Sir Frederick Lewis, Bt. (afterwards Lord Essendon), President of the Chamber of Shipping, 1920.

Sir Charles Sanders, formerly of the Board of Trade.

Sir Leslie Scott, K.C., M.P. (afterwards Lord Justice Scott).

J. Herbert Scrutton, Chairman of Lloyd's Register, 1922.

H. J. Spratt, Secretary of the Chamber of Shipping.

Rt. Hon. Walter Runciman (created Viscount Runciman of Doxford in 1940).

There was no committee to manage the XXI Dining Circle. Usually in consultation with Abell, I invited a guest of distinction to talk to us each evening and summoned the members. We sat round a horse-shoe table, so that there was no chairman. The proceedings were informal; after the guest had spoken, without rising from his seat, the subject was discussed with complete freedom, anyone speaking when he liked to intervene. The Dining Circle continued for several years. The membership underwent a few changes. And then, as I had become preoccupied with other things and Sir Westcott had taken up his appointment as Professor of Naval Architecture at what is now Durham University, it lapsed.

The XXI Dining Circle led to the cementing of a much-valued friendship with Ernest Glover. I had moved into Kent, and it was inconvenient to return home. So Glover frequently became my host at his house overlooking

Hadley Common, a beautiful Georgian place of mellowed red brick, set in charming lawns and gardens. However late we might arrive, Lady Glover, a born hostess, was awaiting us in the drawing-room to hear what had been happening. A link in my life-chain snapped when Glover died suddenly some years later. I realised that I should never have another friend of just the same fine character and experience. His devotion during his work at the Ministry of Shipping shortened his life, and by the time the war was over he had got wound up in work for his local hospital and other causes. Such was his spirit that he gave himself no leisure, but would be busy with his correspondence or accounts most Sunday afternoons after working in London throughout the week, not excluding Saturdays.

Another friendship which was due to my absorption in shipping matters during the war was with a neighbour at Hampstead, Harry Bashford,[1] whose name as the author of "A Corner of Harley Street" and other volumes of much charm is known to a wide public. A doctor by profession, he was marked out for Harley Street, if he had not perversely chosen to enter the medical department of the Post Office, which employs more workers than any business in the country. I knew nothing of medicine. I had not played cricket since a ball nearly put out one of my eyes, while he followed the game with enthusiasm; I had once held a rod in the hope of catching a fish in the Dart, and decided that that sport was not for me, while to him it was an absorbing passion to which he devoted every holiday. We had few interests in common, but we became firm friends. We collaborated in one book which appeared under our joint names, and Bashford, with his acute mind, helped me in writing other books.

He had never read any of the works of Mahan, descriptive of the influence of sea power on history; he had had

[1] Sir Henry Haworth Bashford, M.D., M.R.C.P., Principal Medical Officer of the Post Office.

no experience at sea. But he had an instinctive appreciation of the importance of the Royal Navy and shipping
to a country such as ours—completely surrounded by water,
as we were reminded at school, and also the pivot of a
world-wide Empire, linked together by the sea and dependent upon it for trade. So we talked the same language
which others did not understand, and became friends.
During these years, Bashford was laying the foundations of a most distinguished career in the public
services; at length, he was made Principal Medical Officer
of the General Post Office, with its army of workers
in all parts of these islands; and then, a unique
event in the case of the P.M.O. of the department,
he was knighted.

So the years of my life passed. Before the last volume
of the official history was published I had bought the
Shipping World, and with my retirement from the *Daily
Telegraph* at the end of 1927 a new phase opened. It had
been my ambition to own this weekly paper, which had
been published since 1883. But it had seemed as though
it would never be realised. During the war I cemented a
friendship with Captain W. Bell White, a sailor, a Younger
Brother of Trinity House and a barrister, who had determined to breathe new life into the Worshipful Company of
Shipwrights, one of the most ancient of the City guilds,
which was at the time in a rather moribund condition. He
drew me into his crusade. Before he died, he had the satisfaction of seeing the Duke of York (King George VI) in-
stalled as Permanent Master of the company.

In its affairs His Royal Highness took the deepest interest.
He was usually accompanied to the annual dinner by
the Duchess of York, who also attended a luncheon when
she was made an Honorary Freeman, or should it be Free-
woman? The debt which the company owed to its
Permanent Master and the Duchess was further increased
when, on His Royal Highness ascending the throne, he
decided that he would retain that position, a mark of

gracious interest in the Shipwrights' Company which assured
its future. The gatherings of the shipwrights were held in
the pleasant Barbers' Hall, now substantially destroyed by
German bombing. Everyone who was privileged to come
into association with His Royal Highness there must
retain pleasant memories of his concern for everything
affecting the welfare of the guild and its scholarship funds
for the encouragement of the craft. His presence meant a
journey into the City, but neither he nor the Duchess
seemed to grudge the time or the trouble involved.

At Bell White's suggestion I was made an Honorary Freeman of the Shipwrights' Company in October 1922, being
appointed honorary historian and librarian, practically
sinecure positions. He and I worked together to restore the
prestige of the company. At one of our committee meetings
he suggested that Mr. John Findlay, the editor of and
principal shareholder in the *Shipping World*, should be
invited to join the guild. Incidentally, he mentioned that
Findlay wanted to sell the paper, as he was living for the
greater part of the year in Scotland. In the result, I took
over all the debentures and shares, agreeing that for one
year at least I would make no changes in the staff, and that
I would continue the pension to the former secretary of
the company. I never had reason to regret this adventure
and the undertakings which were part of the bargain.

Thus I became wedded to the shipping and shipbuilding
industries. Mr. James Herbert Scrutton, who had been
vice-president of the Chamber of Shipping (he declined the
presidency) and had filled the responsible position of chairman of Lloyd's Register of Shipping, became my silent
partner. This association proved to be of the happiest
character. Though he never attempted to interfere with
the conduct of the paper, his invaluable advice was always
forthcoming. He had bought an estate in Gloucestershire,
but was frequently in London and therefore was accessible.
When he died he was a member of the Council of the
Institution of Naval Architects.

I was asked by the Council to write an appreciation of his life and work for the "Proceedings" of that body. In doing so I mentioned that he had retired from business in 1930, and recalled that so highly had he been esteemed and so greatly were his experience and judgment valued, that although no longer owning a ship, he was asked to continue to serve on the Council of the Chamber of Shipping. He also served on the General Committee of Lloyd's Register, and remained a member of the London General Shipowners Society, of which he had been chairman in 1905–6. I have counted it one of the greatest strokes of good fortune in my life to have had the wise counsel of such a friend, who completed my education in shipping matters which Westcott Abell had begun. Scrutton's death was a great sorrow to me, but I had happily another wise adviser in my brother Martin, who had helped me in solving the initial problems which the purchase of the *Shipping World* presented to me.

With the acquisition of this paper, together with "The Shipping World Year Book and Port Directory of the World," a new chapter in my life opened. My study of shipping and shipbuilding was made at closer quarters than in the past. I soon realised that British shipping had to be regarded differently from British railways. It is not like the railways, which are nationally circumscribed, but is a branch of an international industry. The seas are all one; ships of all nations use them freely, competing with each other for trade, sometimes with the support of the State, as, for instance, in the case of the United States, Japan, Germany, France and Italy. Under conditions of freedom from State support or control, which existed down to the outbreak of war in 1914, Germany being the only serious rival, British ships carried one-half of the world's ocean-borne trade, including nine-tenths of the inter-Imperial trade, over three-fifths of the trade between the Empire and foreign countries, and nearly one-third of the trade between foreign countries—that is, trade in which British merchants had no concern. Ours was then a proud and profitable position.

Though British shipping has declined since the eve of the war of 1914–18 in face of uneconomic competition, it is still largely engaged in trade between foreign ports. Yet on no trade route, not even the Empire routes, has it any protection against the competition of the shipping of other countries, some of it spoon-fed by the State, and some reflecting far lower standards of living as, for instance, Greece. In these circumstances, the British shipowner conducts an unsheltered industry. To the extent to which he pays the crews more than his rivals and provides them with better food and accommodation, he is handicapped in trying to secure cargoes and, to some extent passengers, in the world market. He is engaged, in short, in an international industry, under a handicap owing to the higher standard of living in this country and the exacting British regulations concerning safety of life and property at sea.

When I came to study the effect of the war on the industry, it was no matter of surprise that it had suffered partial eclipse. The Government made large profits out of the ships it controlled in the latter half of the struggle. It got a rake off of nearly £16,000,000 on the war risk insurance scheme. Many millions were made out of the difference between the contracted rates, called Blue Book rates, at 13s. 6d., which were paid for requisitioned British vessels, and the market rates paid to neutrals, which were as high as 40s., even after the establishment of Inter-Allied Control. Further profits were made by the Government by reletting the ships. Shipowners were also handicapped by the payment of the Excess Profits Duty, which was imposed until 1920, when the industry was about to enter upon a long depression. In a spirit of high adventure, which proved very costly to them, owners bought at peak prices all the new ships which the Government had on its hands when the Peace Treaty was signed. Altogether, in replacing the tonnage which had been lost at sea, they spent

SIR ARCHIBALD HURD BEING WELCOMED *by* ADMIRAL SIR HENRY OLIVER,
COMMANDER-IN-CHIEF, ATLANTIC FLEET

THE SHAW, BRASTED CHART, Nr. SEVENOAKS

£134,000,000 more than the amount they had received under their insurance policies.

The war and post-war policy of the Government, in association with inequitable foreign competition, had brought the industry so low by the end of 1938 that financial aid from the State was recognised as necessary. When the British Shipping (Assistance) Bill was submitted to the House of Commons in July 1939, it was admitted that a case for State assistance had been made out. If it had not been for the profits which were made in the first two years of war of 1914–18—that is before all deep-sea tonnage was requisitioned—the industry would have been nearly bankrupt during the depression of subsequent years, and then we should not have been able to check Germany's policy of aggression in 1939, however anxious we might have been to intervene.

The national importance of the shipping industry is not generally appreciated. As a branch of an international industry, shipping has for many years been the greatest of all our exporting industries; the net shipping earnings in 1920—not the profits—were estimated by the Board of Trade at £300,000,000. These invisible exports helped in the past to balance the national trading account, paying for food and raw materials which we could not otherwise have bought.

Another mistake is to regard shipping as financed and controlled by a little group of financiers who have hazarded their money in the industry. There is much talk of "shipowners" in this sense. But shipowners are merely business men who are the trustees of a great number of investors who have risked their savings in the acquisition of the 2,500 ships which are maintained on the trade routes. It was estimated by Mr. A. W. Kirkcaldy in his book, "British Shipping," that at the beginning of the war of 1914–18, the "book value" of all the ships on the Register of the United Kingdom was about £164,000,000. But that figure excluded all the other property of the industry, which must have run into many more millions. Moreover, shipping cannot be considered without reference to its associated and dependent industries, which are concerned with the building and equipment of ships and their repair, with the docks, warehouses and wharves, and so on.

Mr. C. Ernest Fayle, in his "British Shipping and the War," came to the conclusion that the capital invested in the maritime industries a quarter of a century ago was "not far short of £1,000,000,000." In subsequent years, the figure must have greatly increased, because everything is dearer to-day. But whatever the amount of capital which has been invested in the maritime industries, the idea that it represents the private fortunes of a comparatively few business men, known as shipowners, is beside the mark. Thousands of investors, many of them people of modest means, are interested in the fortunes and misfortunes of the maritime industries.

In the past, capital has been attracted to the industry because anything to do with ships is a bit of a gamble, and therefore is attractive to a race which founded an Empire by taking risks. Sometimes profits are high, and sometimes there are none at all. There are investors who enjoy adventures on the chance of an occasional rich harvest. Whatever "profiteering" there may have been in the early period of the struggle of 1914–18—profits made at world rates to which the industry was entitled—there was none in subsequent years.

When I began to mix with shipowners of the old school and to appreciate their achievements, I realised how sadly popular education, free and compulsory, had failed to produce men of the same self-reliant type. Indeed, one of the most pathetic delusions of the later years of the Victorian period was that compulsory, and, therefore, necessarily free education for everyone would bring about Utopian conditions which would put into the shade More's picture of the ideal State. The delusion became all the more pathetic when agitation resulted in religion being banished to all intents and purposes from the schools

administered by the local authorities. The glorification of
education, whatever its character, as a cure for all the ills
of the body politic led to the creation of a vast machine
which pumps all kinds of unsuitable information into the
children, which they do not and cannot digest. Many of
them leave school hardly able to do more than write their
names; few can spell; their vocabulary is so limited that
they are led to swear uncouth, meaningless words to
emphasise their meaning; while the less said about their
ability to do simple sums the better. But most serious of
all the defects of this education, and the legislation of the
last half century, is that many children grow up with the
conviction that work is a curse instead of a blessing, that the
State should do everything for them, and that if they do not
have a good time the country of which they are citizens has
betrayed them.

It has been my good fortune to know many self-made
men, as they are called. I recall shipowners who served
before the mast, and by their own unaided efforts educated
themselves and established fleets. Sir Walter—afterwards
Lord—Runciman, Sir William Reardon Smith and Sir
Edward Nicholl owed nothing to the State. When I became
friendly with the first named, "the manager of the Moor
Line," of which he was virtual owner, he was advanced in
years, but could use a pen, as the books he wrote proved,
as capably as any journalist. But he remained a sailor at
heart, the champion of the seamen. He found relaxation
on board the yacht *Sunbeam,* which he bought from Lord
Brassey. It was a ship of beauty. It is one of the regrets
of my life that I was never able to take advantage of
repeated invitations to join her on a cruise. But I saw
much of the veteran seaman when my wife and I visited
him in his seaside home at Seahouses, on the Northumbrian
coast. It was an ideal place of rest, from which one looked
out over the sea towards Lindisfarn. After dinner our
host would linger at the table, telling of his early experiences at sea, or he would move into the adjoining room
and lead us in a quarter-deck voice in the singing of

shanties which he loved, and which his nephew, the late
Sir Richard Terry, the musician, preserved for all time.

Lord Runciman, when I knew him, had reached the
conviction that the sun of the Liberal Party was setting.
It could not compete with the Socialists for the votes of
the masses.   One Sunday morning a message was received
that a party was motoring from Doxford, his son's neighbouring estate, and that it included Godfrey Collins, the
whip of the party.   When it arrived, Lord Runciman shook
hands with Collins, saying, "Well, Godfrey, I heard you
were coming, and I have had my pockets sewn up."   He
was, I think, the most sagacious of men I ever knew, and
his judgment was usually unerring.   His pride in the rapid
rise in the political world of his only son, of whose success
he had never had a doubt, increased year by year, but it
was never forced upon his visitors.   They sat in the House
of Commons simultaneously, the son as Minister and the
father as a private member.   One day a friend of mine
came across the owner of the Moor Line in the Lobby, in
none too good a temper.   "What's the matter, Sir Walter?"
he asked.   "I had prepared a speech," was the answer, "and
Walter wouldn't let me make it."   It was a great grief to
all his friends when the master of so many ships lost his
wife, a charming hostess who had been his companion in
storm and sunshine for so many years, often going to sea
with him in their early married life.   She died after a
long illness.

Though from this time onwards I turned my thoughts to
shipping, I retained my interest in naval affairs, and in fact
became once more closely associated with the Navy League.
Soon after moving to London, I had joined the executive
committee at a time when the life and soul of the League
was "Pat Hannon," [1] as he was known to everyone in those
days.   After leaving the Royal University of Ireland, he
had devoted his gifts as speaker and organiser to Irish
agriculture, had then done much the same work for the
South African Government, and having returned to England

[1] Sir Patrick Hannon, M.P. since 1921 for the Moseley Division of
Birmingham.

in 1910, he had joined the executive of the Navy League. A year later he became its General Secretary and editor of *The Navy*. Hannon was a dynamic personality, and he made it his task to breathe life into the dry bones of this moribund organisation. It was an inspiration to work with him. But when, on his retirement, the Navy League became indoctrinated with the ideas of the League of Nations Union, a comic situation for such a patriotic educational organisation, I retired. From the time that the United States had decided to have nothing to do with the League of Nations, I had concluded that it could do no good.

Later, when Admiral G. O. Stephenson became the secretary of the Navy League, I rejoined the executive committee, and was a member of it during the period when, as president,[1] Lord Lloyd devoted his great powers to the revival of its fallen fortunes. The amount of thought and time which he gave to this task filled me with admiration, as he had many other interests in life. He realised that our future was on the sea, as our past had been. He succeeded in reviving the Navy League in face of many obstacles, for the public had lost interest in the Royal Navy. At one meeting of the committee, a lady member told us of the difficulty which was being experienced in getting volunteers to sell flags on Navy Flag Day, as some of them had been treated so contemptuously and rudely in the streets.

Owing to Lord Lloyd's enthusiasm and influence, large funds were collected, Lord Nuffield being a munificent donor towards the expansion of the Sea Scouts movement. The Navy League, with Paymaster-Commander Bishop as general secretary, became once more a potent force, not only in this country, but in the Dominions. When the war opened in 1939, Lord Lloyd could regard the awakening of public opinion and the revival of the strength of the Fleet as being in no small measure due to the educational work which had been carried on under his leadership.

[1] Lord Lloyd became Secretary of State for the Colonies in 1939.

CHAPTER X

THE FAITH OF AN ISLANDER

WHEN Bleriot flew the English Channel in thirty-one minutes in July 1909 and landed triumphantly on the cliff near Dover, it was said that Britain was no longer an island. But this event did not change the geographical fact that this country is completely surrounded by water. It is still essential, as we are so dependent, on the one hand, on overseas supplies of food and raw materials, and, on the other, on the sale of our manufactures to pay for our purchases, that the sea communications with the world's markets should be kept open. The peril of starvation remains as great as ever.

Our sure shield again invasion, as distinct from raids, is now, as in the past, the Royal Navy. The martello towers on the Channel coast, the Hythe military canal and other preparations to resist the enemy in the Napoleonic period, are evidence of our ancestors' anxiety. Thomas Hardy, in his Wessex novel "The Trumpet Major," describes the alarm which prevailed along the coast from Dover to Weymouth. After the naval revival of the Victorian era, and before the appearance of the aeroplane, the Admiralty gave a guarantee against invasion in force, and in fact during the war of 1914–18 all the trained troops were sent overseas—to France, the Dardanelles, Egypt and Palestine.

This country relied for three years and more on the Navy, and the Navy only. Even in those circumstances, the Germans were wise enough not to attempt invasion. The only change in the situation that has since occurred is that limited numbers of enemy soldiers can be transported by air; but the fate of such men would not be uncertain.

On the other hand, "The Battle of Britain" in the autumn of 1940 showed that the development of air power had robbed us, for the time at least, of freedom from *any* form of attack upon our cities and towns.   But so long as we maintain adequate defences on the coast, such as were always necessary in the past, as well as inland, where small numbers of parachutists might land from planes, no vital change has occurred to threaten our security.

In war, air raids by an enemy can inflict heavy loss of life, possibly greater than the carnage on the roads arising from the careless driving of motor-cars; houses, churches, hospitals and even munition works may be blasted by bombs.   But, unless history can no longer be regarded as a guide, the carefully planned defensive will in time overtake the offensive of " hit or miss " bombing.   In any event, such attacks cannot render unnecessary the watch and ward of the Fleet, or the coming and going of merchant ships with their cargoes of imports and exports under its protection. As a French historian has remarked, "A stoppage in Britain's trade circulation would be the equivalent of an embolism in the human blood-stream."

An islander, living in a small country largely devoted to manufacturing goods for home consumption and export overseas, must have a different outlook on life from the man who lives on a continent, hemmed in not by the sea, but by the frontiers of other countries, potential enemies. To such an islander sea power is the barrier against seaborne invasion and starvation. Sea power is not a matter merely of ships or of seamen, but of national environment and national will, instinct with an appreciation of the benefits, political, economic and social, which can be obtained by the wise use of the sea. Some people think of sea power in terms of ships of war and others in terms of ships of commerce, but these are complementary. If the one type of ship, the ship of war, is ignored, the other type of ship, the merchant ship will, in the present condition of the world, inevitably disappear.

13

And more important than the skilfully manipulated steel ships are the seamen, our first-line defenders and the suppliers of all we need of the riches of the world.

Human nature has not changed in the past 1,000 years. In spite of all the talking at innumerable conferences, this country's overseas supplies still depend upon our ability to ensure safe transport by sea; the greater the safety, the cheaper the food, owing to the low freights demanded by the shipowner and the modest charge for the insurance of ships and cargoes.

Whenever I pass the statue of Alfred the Great at the bottom of the main street of Winchester, with a green hill rising behind it, I feel inclined to raise my hat in salute to his spirit. He discovered the miracles which could be performed by sea power. This country, overrun by virile neighbours from across the North Sea, was apparently destined to become the subject state of a continental power. The inhabitants, without a fleet, could not protect themselves; they never knew at what point on the long coastline an invader would land. Alfred realised that the invader had to be challenged and defeated by sea, and not by land. It was by carrying into effect that doctrine that he assured to his subjects the privilege of living their own lives and working out their own national existence. "There is no advantage in living on an island," he declared, "unless your navy rides in undisputed sway over the waters that surround it."

The making of England, guarded and protected by its seamen, was a long business, because sea consciousness was of sluggish growth in these islands. Men were fascinated by the sight of many soldiers in the panoply of war. Appreciation of the vital importance of sea power developed slowly, behind sea bulwarks which ensured freedom from continental interference.

The people of the British Isles had first to become masters of themselves before they could be fitted to become masters of others. They had made some headway in governing themselves by the time Queen Elizabeth came to the throne. The seeds of British sea power, which found expression in freedom of thought, speech and action, had been sown. The Elizabethans, with a sure mastery of the sea, engaged in what may be regarded as exploratory work, realising that over the horizon lay other lands with which they might trade with profit, and wherein they might plant those liberal institutions they had themselves created in their own land. But as Professor Seely has reminded us, "In the last years of Queen Elizabeth, England had absolutely no possession outside Europe, for all schemes of settlement, from that of Hore in Henry VIII's time to those of Gilbert and Raleigh, had failed. Great Britain did not yet exist; Scotland was a separate kingdom, and in Ireland the English were but a colony in the midst of an alien population, still in the tribal state." [1]

In these years of the making of England, the truth was established that *the sea controls the land*. As Raleigh put it, "Whosoever commands the sea, commands the trade; whosoever commands the trade of the world, commands the riches of the world, and consequently the world itself." The history books used in our schools need rewriting. The important event in our early history was not the struggle of the native inhabitants with the disciplined Romans after they had landed, but the uncontested landing of the Romans on these shores, of which the historian tells us little or nothing. The Battle of Hastings was the sequel to the mischance which forced Harold to withdraw his fleet from the English Channel, first, to the Thames owing to shortage of food and the need for repairs, and, secondly, further North to resist his brother Tostig's descent on the East Coast of England. It was the unopposed landing of William the Conqueror which decided the history of England for succeeding centuries. So long as the Channel was held by the invader, with one foot in England and the other in Normandy, England was little more than a colony. It was the failure of sea power which at last brought the Nor-

[1] "The Expansion of England."

mans, who had been little more than visitors to England, face
to face with the necessity of choosing whether to return
home or to remain in this island. Many of them remained
and did not do badly by settling here.

And so on from century to century down to the defeat
of the Armada, the decisive events were not the battles
fought on land, except in so far as our internal development
was concerned, but the decisive or indecisive actions by
sea. At every crisis in British history, it was proved that
the sea controls the land.

Our prestige to-day rests on sea power. Lloyd's is the
marine insurance market of the whole world; German is
the language of Science, French is the language of
Diplomacy, but English is the language of the Sea. When
the International Shipping Conference met after the war
of 1914–18 in London, although delegates from all parts
of the world attended it, the proceedings were conducted
throughout in English. No interpreter was necessary.
Foreigners come to the Court of Admiralty to settle maritime disputes rather than resort to a foreign court of law;
the Baltic is the chartering market of the sea-trading nations.

We owe the predominance of the English people in all
maritime affairs to the enterprise of the Elizabethan sailors
and their successors. They had the seaman's skill, the
merchant's mind, the acquisitive instinct, but they had also
liberal sentiments which had found expression in their own
order of life.

From the time of the first charter given to Virginia in
1606, the civilising work in the world, initiated by
Elizabethan seamen, went on. It made some advance in
the seventeenth century, but not until the next century
had the doctrine of sea power been thoroughly digested.
The expansion of England then became a great liberalising
force in the world. The struggle for the freedom of the
sea, and all it implied in liberty, reached its climax in the
early years of last century, when Napoleon was defeated, in
the main, by the exertions of the islanders of this country.

British sea power has time and again been opposed to foreign military power. What has military power achieved? Every ruler who has aspired to dominate the continent of Europe has evolved, by pressure of military arms, a war-map suggestive of victory. Philip II of Spain became the dictator of the destinies of the nations of the Old and the New Worlds in virtue of the victories achieved by his troops under Cortes, Pizarro and Palma; his war-map was to be a monument for all time. Louis XIV was enabled to impose his will on his neighbours owing to the success which attended his armies over a long series of years; he possessed, as a thing of consuming pride, his war-map. Napoleon, in the opening years of last century, had practically the whole Continent at his feet; his war-map suggested to him that he was "Emperor of the West." Never before had the value of military power been so conspicuously exhibited as during the decade which separated Trafalgar from Waterloo. Whatever errors Napoleon might commit, it seemed as though Fate were ready to annul the consequences and assist him in placing Europe under his heel. He passed from conquest to conquest. He was encouraged to distribute thrones among his family and his suite. The old order was seemingly disappearing; wherever a nominee of Napoleon's did not reign, there was to be found some royal vassal who, willing or unwilling, paid homage to the master of the *Grand Armée*.

Who outside these islands believed at that stage of Napoleonic radiance that Europe was the witness of nothing more than a passing phase of reaction, and that already unseen forces were at work which would bring to nothing the vast political structure, to the creation of which Napoleon devoted his genius? Even Pitt exclaimed after the Battle of Austerlitz, " Roll up the map of Europe ; it will not be wanted these ten years." Within a few years the *debacle* came. The man who had been overlord of Europe became a prisoner on board a British battleship, and thus passed to St. Helena, to live the remainder of his days not even master in the modest villa which provided him with shelter from the inclemencies of nature and the anger of man. He exhibited the imagination, genius and the driving power of a devil and the restraining capacity of a statesman. He could gain victories on land and he could consolidate them, winning to his standard those whom he had conquered. And yet he failed. He was never master of the sea.

In the war of 1914–18 German arms met with success after success on land; the enemy had his war-map. The Kaiser could point to military victories, the harvest of thirty years of persistent, extravagant and purposeful preparation to assert Prussian domination over Europe. The Germans held Belgium in slavery; the whole of Northern France was in their grip; unhappy Poland had once more experienced the horrors of invasion; Courland had been wrenched from the feeble hands of revolutionary Russia; the King and Government of Rumania had been evicted; Serbia and Montenegro had been overrun; Italy had been invaded. The German Army, moving on interior lines, had lunged first in one direction and then in another, and everywhere except on the West, where the British Army intervened, supported by overwhelmingly strong sea power, a large measure of success was achieved. Prussianism was supreme. The Berlin machine had not failed in the eyes of the German people; victory had succeeded victory in quick succession; but every success had been purchased at a higher price than Napoleon ever paid. And yet final success was still wanting!

It is of interest, in passing, to note the difference between the two pictures of war furnished by an examination of the characters of Napoleon and the German Kaiser. The former was a giant—a great ruler and administrator as well as a great soldier, possibly the greatest soldier of modern times. His contemporaries have left us a record of the thoughts which chased each other through his mind during his years of captivity. One day he took up one of the year-books of his reign. "It was a fine Empire," he mused; "I ruled eighty-three millions of human beings, more than half the population of Europe;" but he reflected that history would scarcely mention him because he was "overthrown." "Had I been able to maintain my dynasty, it had been different." The captive did not realise the deep mark, permanent and inerasable, which he had left on the world's history. He saw only the ruin of his military dreams, and he was unconscious of the influence which his respect for law and his admiration for settled and, in some measure, liberal government was to exert for many years after he had passed away. But he realised at last that he had been defeated by the invincible British Navy.

Until comparatively recent times an army was regarded in this country with suspicion, since it might attempt to dictate to the nation, while the Fleet has been looked upon with favour. The Navy goes on from century to century, but since the Commonwealth each successive Government has had to receive authority from Parliament year by year to maintain the Army. Down to quite recent times, this national sentiment was reflected in our defensive policy. Our forefathers looked upon the Army as a force to be used in an emergency merely as an extension of our sea power—a spearhead, finely tempered, to be thrust at any enemy at the point where he least expected attack, for movement by sea is less conspicuous than movement by land. The element of surprise is an important factor in all operations by sea.

Until the Great War of 1914–18, this country had never attempted to raise a great army. Admiral Saunders took across the Atlantic only a small military force to hand over to Wolfe, that he might conquer Canada. Wellington commanded forces which might now be placed under a Brigadier. British troops fought on the Continent, of course, many times, but always in restricted numbers. This country, strong in its sea power, got into the habit of supplementing its military strength by subsidising allies, who were willing to fight with us—at a price. One historian has recorded: "The

marvel of Wellington's career of victory, which began in
Portugal and ended at Waterloo, is that he never had under
his command any large number of British troops. The first
expedition to Portugal was only 30,000 strong. Of the
100,000 he commanded in the campaign of Vittoria, of the
68,000 he set in array on the ridge of Mont St. Jean, only a
third were British. In Spain his numbers were swelled by
Germans, Spaniards and Portuguese. At Waterloo, German,
Dutch and Belgian regiments made up two-thirds of the
battle line."

Ten years, in which we engaged in many military adventures on the continent of Europe, separated Trafalgar from
Waterloo. A French writer has said that "they were the
ships of Nelson that won the Battle of Waterloo." An
American—Mahan—in commenting on the Battle of
Trafalgar, has declared that "Amid all the pomp and
circumstance of war, which for ten years to come desolated
the Continent, amid all the tramping to and fro over
Europe of the French armies and their auxiliary legions,
there went on unceasingly the noiseless pressure upon the
vitals of France, that compulsion whose silence, when once
noted, becomes to the observer the most striking and awful
mark of the working of sea power." Sea power is always
active, but there are few decisive actions at sea, and that is
what so many people do not realise. They want battles,
and they do not get them and are disappointed.

If the defeat of the Spanish Armada may be regarded as
this country's assertion of its right to live its life in its
own way, the defeat of the French and their Allies in the
Napoleonic Wars may be regarded as notice by the British
people to the world that, as they lived in freedom, so they
intended that other people in other and far distant lands
should also live. From the time of Waterloo, we settled down
to the task of making, extending and consolidating the
British Empire on lines quite unlike those of any empire
which had gone before—because it was founded by islanders,
drawing their inspiration from the sea.

During the centuries of empire making, as during the period of nation making, this country never wielded anything more than an army contemptible in size. In the latter half of the eighteenth century it never reached 100,000 men, and in some years was below 20,000 men. At the time of the Crimean War it stood, after superhuman efforts to expand it, at no more than 222,874 men. Contrast this record with the experience of 1914–18. This country and the Overseas Empire put into the various theatres of war about 10,000,000 men. The British peoples made that breakaway from their traditional maritime policy owing to the initial failure of our Allies, volatile and restless France and lumbering and blundering Russia. With the support of the British Fleet, they should have been able to crush the Central Powers as easily as we crack a nut. They failed, and we went to their rescue, raising a vast army. We did more than supply naval and military power.

When the struggle was over, economists and statesmen put forward many explanations of our subsequent distress. They were all wrong. Having provided, as a sure foundation of our war effort, a fleet stronger than the next strongest fleet in the world, that of Germany, we built up an enormous army, lent our Allies many millions of pounds, supplied them with food, carried their cargoes for them by sea and converted this country into a vast munition factory. We overstrained our man power, our purses and our hearts, and hence the long illness which ensued, with widespread unemployment and distress.

The influence of sea power explains the making of England and the building up of the British Empire. What we call the British Empire—an unfortunate term—is incurably maritime. It is the conspicuous fruit of British sea power. It embraces nearly one-quarter of the land surface of the globe, with a population of about 500,000,000. Only 60,000,000 of these people are of British origin, and the rest are native born. If we have controlled the destinies of all these millions of ebony, chocolate, mahogany or yellow

14

peoples, we have not done so by an army. Even in India we have kept only about 65,000 soldiers—65,000 soldiers in a country larger than the continent of Europe (excluding Russia), inhabited by a population of upwards of 300,000,000 people.

The British triumph lies, however, not so much in the conquest of many million of square miles of territory, as in the planting of liberal principles in these distant parts of the world. The white man has hitherto been in the ascendant, but stage by stage, with his back always to the sea, with its reserves of strength, the conqueror, in accordance with our sea-born principles, has been sharing in increasing measure the conqueror's privileges as well as the conqueror's responsibilities with the conquered. The conquered are obtaining a larger and larger share in the life of the most virile League of Nations which has ever existed. The existence of this Commonwealth of peace-loving and freedom-enjoying nations is evidence of the virtues that flow from sea power.

Many years ago that most active Imperial statesman and sailor, Admiral Colomb, asked, "What is the British Empire in its maritime aspect?" He answered the question in the following words:

It is a vast, straggling, nervous, arterial and venous system, having its heart, lungs and brain in the British Islands, its alimentary bases in the great possessions of India, Australia and North America, and its ganglia in the Crown Colonies.

Through this system pulsates the life-blood of the Empire. Main arteries and corresponding veins lead east through the Mediterranean and the Red Sea to India, China and Australia; west to America and the West Indies; south to Australia, Southern Africa, and America and to the Pacific. Capillaries the most minute, at the extremities of civilisation, gather up the raw produce of the nations, transmit it to the larger channels, which in their turn convey it to the heart. This tremendous organ, having extracted all that is necessary for its own sustenation, forces the transmitted produce through the great main channels, and finally through millions of branching filaments to sustain and revivify the nations of the earth to their remotest borders.

The life of an Empire so highly organised must hang by a thread. It is no mollusc from whose inert substance huge masses may be detached at will without much effect upon its vitality. It is a living organism whose parts are all interdependent, and highly sensitive in their relations. A stab at the heart may put it to death more suddenly, but perhaps not more surely, than the severing of a remote artery, or the wound of a "nerve centre."

Wherever we, as islanders, have gone we have planted, not only the British flag, but the principles of government by which we have ourselves developed, and in which we still place our trust. It is called democracy under a limited monarchy. The monarchy may at times seem too limited, and the democracy too unlimited. But, at any rate, throughout the British Empire the democratic rule of life exists, ranging from the complete freedom of the Dominions, down through the evolutionary stage of the Colony to that of the Protectorate. The freedom which the sea has inspired in us we are sharing more and more with those who are partners with us in the greatest and most hopeful of all national experiments.

What has been the influence of British sea power on other nations? The characteristic of British sea power is that it is neither domineering nor selfish. We have desired to share its blessings with the world. Believing in our own habit of life, we have been insistent—sometimes, it is true, at the point of the gun—that others should enjoy similar blessings. I suggest that the historian has underestimated the beneficial influence which British sea power has exerted on the world at large. He sometimes pays grudging tribute to its influence on the fortunes of the British peoples. But then he hesitates.

A year or two before his death, Admiral Mahan reviewed the development of American policy since the acquisition of the Philippines, and remarked on the gradual, yet perpetual, process by which a higher civilisation impinges

upon a lower; that is, upon one that is lower in virile
efficiency, however, in some instances, it may have been
higher in acquired material comfort, or even in literary or
artistic achievement. Continuing his line of argument, he
remarked:

Why do English innate political conceptions of popular
representative government, of the balance of law and
liberty, prevail in North America from the Arctic Circle
to the Gulf of Mexico, from the Atlantic to the Pacific?
Because the command of the sea at the decisive era
belonged to Great Britain.

In India and Egypt administrative efficiency has taken
the place of a welter of tyanny, feudal struggle and blood-
shed, achieving thereby the comparative welfare of the
once harried populations. What underlies this administrative efficiency? The British Navy, assuring in the first
instance British control instead of French, and thereafter
communication with the home country, whence the local
power without which administration everywhere is futile.

What, at the moment the Monroe doctrine was proclaimed, insured beyond peradventure the immunity from
foreign oppression of the Spanish-American colonies in their
struggle for independence? The command of the sea by
Great Britain, backed by the feeble Navy, but imposing
strategic position, of the United States, with her swarm
of potential commerce destroyers, which a decade before
had harassed the trade of even the mistress of the seas.

Wherever on the map we recognise a free nation which
has come to birth in the last 300 years or so, history
records that we as islanders, with our ships of war and our
ships of commerce, have had a hand in shaping its destiny.
Portugal is free because she has been our Ally since
Henry VII's time; Greece would never have become a
nation if it had not been for the British Fleet; Mussolini
would never have had a United Italy to dominate if it
had not been for British sea power.

As islanders we owe our pre-eminence in commerce, in
the main, to sea power. The day has gone by when
merchants were adventurers, placing their goods on board

their own ships and setting forth in the frail craft as commercial travellers, thereby risking their lives as well as their property in order to find buyers. There are no finer pages of sea romance than the lives of such pioneer merchant adventurers as in past centuries sailed from London, Bristol, Liverpool and other ports to discover new markets. They had their share in spreading the sea-derived liberal principles in other lands. Because of them, we became the carriers of the world.

In the past 100 years the population of this country has trebled. The explanation is to be found in the wise use of sea power, first in ensuring freedom from invasion, and secondly, in bringing to our shores the riches of the world. As we grew in numbers, we found that we could draw on other nations for our necessities, owing to the efficiency, and, above all, the cheapness, of sea carriage. Land transport is about ten times as costly as sea transport. There is not a town of any industrial importance in this country which is more than 70 miles from the sea, so the food and raw materials which its inhabitants buy, and the coal or manufactures which they sell, have only a short and costly land journey. Of all nations, we as islanders have, therefore, gained the greatest benefits from sea power.

Before the war opened in September 1939, ships were carrying wheat and other grain cargoes many thousands of miles at rates which worked out at barely one penny per quarter for every hundred miles. That meant that sufficient wheat for 120 loaves of 4 lb. each was carried thousands of miles at a charge of one penny. Meat, fruit and other perishable foods were being brought in expensive refrigerated ships from Australia and New Zealand, from South Africa and Argentina, and from California and British Columbia at rates of freight at which neither the railways nor the road transport companies could look for a hundredth part of the distance. It cost more to carry British produce a few miles from the producer to the consumer than it did to bring overseas produce from the other side of the world, so disproportionate to the distance was the charge for sea and land carriage. Lord Fisher summed up his faith, as I would sum my own, in the words of William Watson:

> God and the Ocean and some favouring Star
> In high cabal, have made us what we are.

As this country must have a supreme Fleet, so it must have a supreme Merchant Navy. Shipping is an essential industry to an island people, who must import most of their food and raw materials, and, in order that they may pay for these necessities, *must* export goods and coal. The fact is that the people of the British Isles, whose sea instinct has been developed by their environment, are sea-dependent to a greater extent than any other populations, and, indeed, the whole of the countries forming the British Empire are, in varying degree, also sea-dependent. As an American once remarked: " The component parts of the British Empire are tied together by ships. The component parts of the United States are tied together by railways and highways. Herein lies the essential difference in political importance of commercial shipping in the first two maritime countries." Ships to us in England are not *luxuries*, but *necessities*.

Unconscious of the fruits of sea power, we sat back with folded hands in the years following the Peace of Versailles, while the British Fleet, the first line of defence of the British peoples, was cut down, and while British merchant ships were driven off the seas by the subsidised vessels of other countries. The awakening came, and happily it did not come too late. What of the future? Can it be for the good of the world that the British Fleet, which has charted the seas of the world, suppressed piracy, and made the seas free and safe to all, should be cut down once more, and that British merchant shipping, which has been the principal agency in developing international trade, should have to fight, without aid, against heavy odds for continued existence?

Our need of sea power in future will be greater than

ever. Since British sea power won its triumphs, the
research worker and the scientists have been at work. If
these conspirators had never existed, life to-day in this
country, and, indeed, throughout the world, I suggest,
would be easier, safe, more comfortable and happier than
it is. We have only to read the stories of Richardson,
Fielding, Dickens, Jane Austen, Thackeray and Anthony
Trollope to form some conception of the pleasant conditions
under which men and women—at any rate, many men and
women—worked and lived before the scientist and the
engineer and the chemist had done their deadly work, con-
tracting the time distances of the world to our injury as an
island, and increasing the speed of communications. If
only James Watt had left the tea kettle alone, and Faraday
had adopted his father's trade as a blacksmith, and others
of an inquisitive turn of mind had been content to go
along the beaten track, we should still be living in a land
completely surrounded by water, with all the comfortable
implications which that condition suggests. Practically
every invention for the past hundred years has involved a
limitation of our liberties, a change in our manner of
living owing to the advance of industrialism, an increasing
embroilment in the affairs of other peoples, and an abridg-
ment of our sea power as an island people.

The craze for quicker and more frequent communications
has brought us cheek by jowl with other nations, with
whom our forefathers had hardly a nodding acquaintance.
It was said that improved means of travel and communication would convert all the widely separated nations into
one great friendly family. That dream has been dispelled
by events. The aeroplane, in particular, has been a curse
and not a blessing. Who can take pride in tanks, or gas
masks, or air-raid shelters? In spite of all these develop-
ments, we shall do well, in this country as well as in the
Overseas Empire, to hold fast to the sea faith of our forefathers. "It is hard to say," Gladstone remarked in his
younger days, "whether, or when, our countrymen will be

fully alive to the vast advantages they derive from the consummate means of naval defence combined with our position as an island" (and, he might have said, not only of naval defence, but of trading); and he added that "when the Almighty grants exceptional and peculiar benefits, He sometimes permits, by way of counterpoise, an insensibility to their value."

This little island is "home," the sweetest word in our common language, to thousands of Americans, none the less proud of their British descent because they are themselves citizens of the United States, as well as to millions of men and women in the Dominions, Colonies and Protectorates, within the wide-sweeping orbit of the British Empire. They do not forget that the seeds of civilisation were sown throughout the world by the sparse population of this little island set in the Northern Seas. Though they may, and do, criticise us from time to time, the bonds of blood and descent and tradition count for much. Our kinsmen are proud to claim, as they are entitled to claim, their share in the great achievements of the race.

We have one consolation as we face the future. With the passage of time, the power of the ship has increased because every weapon of violence must be useless unless oil fuel can be obtained, and by the dispensation of providence, the greatest sources of oil supply are far removed from peoples who are in the habit of making war. Apart from comparatively small supplies in Europe, oil for the ships of war, the mechanised armies and the armadas of the air must be ocean-borne. Thus it is the fact that the sea not only controls the land, but it controls also the air. If those who control the oil supplies of the world were to meet in conclave and agree not to supply oil to an aggressor nation, stigmatised as such by some international authority, their word would be more effective than any treaties, or indeed, than any League of Nations, however wisely such a body might be constituted, and however powerfully its decrees might be supported by super-armies, super-navies and super-air forces.

CHAPTER XI

PEACE IN THE COUNTRY

THE country is the place for childhood—first as well as second childhood. After forty years in tumultous cities and towns, I returned to the countryside, where I had been born, though not to the same county.

Do we appreciate as fully as we should do the significance of the country in early life? "God made the country and man made the town." In the country a child's mind develops slowly but surely as its body grows. And the country is the place for second childhood. When the fierce battle of life is over, when victory has been won or defeat suffered, Nature can offer consolations for the years which the locusts have eaten. The silence of the country at night, broken only by the sounds of animals and birds, which are often disturbing to the man or woman who has spent many years amid the jarring noises of town, exerts its healing influence. Great cities are never at rest; the beat of life ceases neither by night or day. The hurry and confusion may add a zest to existence when one is strong and vigorous, but in the sunset years the longing is for peace. That is to be found only in the country, where Nature is always at work, in accordance with laws as old as the world itself, but at work without rush or commotion. "Nature," as Emerson once declared, "never hurries: atom by atom she achieves her work." Things happen in the country naturally; in cities and towns man makes them happen, and in doing so uses up the tissues of his body and exhausts his mind.

Such thoughts as these passed through my mind after the Great War had reached its inevitable end in the triumph of sea power. My wife and I decided that we would live in the country, but within easy reach of London with its mental stimulus, to which we had become accustomed. And thus, owing to a chance week-end visit many years ago, we bought some land on a wooded hillside above a little Kentish village which is not marked on most maps.

There I realised my ambition to build a cottage home which I called "The Shaw," a word which means a small wood, its bricks made in the district, but thatched with reeds from Norfolk. As a precaution against fire, I decided that there should be an under-roof of asbestos sheeting; the architect, Mr. Oswald P. Milne, carried the chimneys high up above the thatch without spoiling the appearance of the cottage. He showed in every detail mastery of the art he practised. As my elder daughter, Vivyen, and her husband, Donald Bremner, also wanted a home in the country, I built a duplicate cottage for them, separated only by a tennis lawn. These two cottages have since grown, as everything has a way of doing in the country. As they have been extended, additional woods have been added to the few acres I bought when first I determined to change my manner of life.

The country is not the place in which to idle, except for the town dweller who needs rest of mind and body so that he may regain his strength and go back refreshed to his daily round. Unless you have occupation, you will soon be bored, for the beauty of nature palls after a time, and not a very long time either. Active work for the mind or hand is necessary, and to find it becomes the first problem to be solved on migrating to some village away from the busy haunts of men, especially if your zest for open-air sport has gone or you have reached the fifth or perhaps the sixth age of man—"the lean and slippered pantaloon, with spectacles on nose and pouch on side." It is too late to begin life again and hunt or shoot or fish, or even to sit on the local bench or take part in the affairs of the county, rural or parish council. One is too old, I found, to begin such work.

My problem was solved for me because I had to make a garden. That is one of the penalties, or blessings, of building a house, whether in a wood or a meadow. One inherits nothing from a predecessor in title except earth. In my case I had nothing but unfriendly acid soil, thick undergrowth and oak scrub broken here and there by uprising beech or firs. The wood where the two cottages were to be built had been cut for hop-poles every seven years, and this particular part of it had a stunted appearance. It was a miniature jungle. When we sought for suitable sites for the cottages, we had sometimes to go on our hands and knees. The ground fell away sharply into a deep valley, and then rose to a well-clad hill. The hillside on which my own cottage stands suggested difficulties in garden making, for soil for roses and most herbaceous plants would have to be imported. What kind of garden should it be, one which would not cost too much money in the making or in the upkeep? That was our problem.

Once the foundations had been dug, revealing a layer of peat over what I was told was "assic," which would grow nothing, it was obvious that all thought of developing an orthodox garden, with neat lawns, gravel paths, rose beds and lily ponds had to be abandoned. The only hope rested in such shrubs and plants as liked, or at least did not dislike, peat. My thoughts immediately turned to rhododendrons, azaleas, kalmias, pernettyas, acers and hypericums. Then by chance I came across a catalogue of the firm of Maxwell & Beale, of Broadstone in Dorsetshire, with twenty pages or so of brief particulars of different kinds of heather. I read that heathers from all parts of the continent of Europe and, indeed, the world, had been brought to this country and propagated and crossed. They would flower in succession the round of the year. And thus it came about that very slowly, over a period of twenty years, I made a garden that is never without bloom. There is never a time when it is bare of some bright colour.

We live our lives as peacefully as the dictators will permit on this hillside, among the pines and beeches and birches, not to mention the gorse, bracken and heather, each with a glory of its own in due season. Though we are out of the main stream of life, we time our watches and clocks by Greenwich, and we get our news, hot and fresh, over the wireless. Some of our menfolk go to London every morning and return in the evening. They tell us country people the news of the great capital of the British Empire, where a man does not know his neighbour, though he may live next door to him for many years. But we are not envious. We have many compensations, whether we be young or old.

INDEX

A

Abell, Sir Westcott, 165, 180–1
Admiralty, 44, 59, 70–1, 120
Air Arm, Fleets', 119
Army strength, 201
Asquith, Rt. Hon. H. H., 5, 46, 82, 88–92, 94, 96, 100–1, 104; on War Book, 84; supports naval increases, 88–91

B

Bacon, Admiral Sir Reginald, 62, 130, 152; the Dover Patrol, 143–6
Balfour, Lord, 44, 79–81, 137, 141, 163; inspires Committee of Imperial Defence, 83; tribute to Churchill, 119; becomes First Lord Admiralty, 159
Barbers Hall, 184
Bashford, Sir H. H., 182–3
Battenberg, Prince Louis of, 70, 123–5, 130, 150
Beatty, Admiral of the Fleet Earl, 48, 54, 130, 146; commands Grand Fleet, 147
Bell, Walter G., 31
Bentley, E. C., 38
Beresford, Admiral Lord Charles, 93–6, 139
Berkeley, village, castle and celebrities, 15
Birkenhead, Earl of, 49–52; speech at Carlton Club, 52
Blucher sunk, 73
Bonar Law, 163
Bowles, Gibson, M.P., 71
Bremner, Vivyen and Donald, 210
Bridge, Admiral Sir Cyprian, on Naval War Staff, 103–4
Burnham, Edward Lawson, Lord, 18, 27, 30, 32, 34, 72
Burnham, Harry Lawson, Viscount, 18, 33–6, 47, 56–9

C

Callaghan, Admiral Sir G., 125, 130
Camrose, Lord, 57–8
Carson, Lord, 138
Chamberlain, Joseph, on coffin ships, 167
Chatfield, Admiral of the Fleet Sir E., 53
Childers, First Lord, 92
Churchill, Rt. Hon. Winston, 49, 130, 139, 144, 163; becomes First Lord, 44, 104, 115; a troubled interview, 44–8; sets up Naval Staff, 115–7; secures oil for Navy, 118; introduces Naval Air Force, 119; strengthening the Fleet, 121–2; leaves Admiralty in 1915, 49, 156; appoints Tank Committee, 157; Prime Minister, 158–9
Clark, Capt. Sir G., 55–6
Clarke, Sir Edward, 54–5
Colomb, Admiral, 202
Committee of Imperial Defence, 81–3
Coronal disaster, 150–1
Country life, 209–12
Courtney, W. L., 31

D

Daily Mail, 29, 30
Daily Telegraph, 18, 26–7, 33–9, 45, 53, 55, 57–8, 86, 98, 104; " young lions " replaced, 30–1; " a happy ship," 32, 37–9
Daniel, Col. E. Y., 83, 135–6
Dardanelles Expedition, 152–6
Dreadnought ships, 62; 73–6, 96; launch of original Dreadnought, 74; first captain, 144; super-Dreadnoughts, 92
Duff, Admiral Sir Alexander, 138–9
Dunraven, Lord, 44

E

Edward VII, King, 67–8, 74–5, 94, 98
Elizabeth, Queen, 183–4
Enchantress, yacht, 48

23

4/3 glove 60